When We Meet Again

An Everlasting Bond That
Transcends the Physcial

R M   B R Y A N T

PAGE PUBLISHING, INC.
Conneaut Lake, PA

First originally published by Page Publishing 2020

ISBN 978-1-6624-0217-3 (pbk)
ISBN 978-1-6624-0218-0 (digital)

Printed in the United States of America

I dedicate this story to my beloved, Jake,
and to all those who have assisted
me on this wonderful and loving journey.
To those who do not see beyond, to those
who never look to see, to those who don't
want to see, and to those who never have
to see but yet still believe.
For my Jake who has confirmed and
brought me renewed knowledge,
belief, comfort, and intense love.
I thank him,
for he has set my spirit free!

I am but a shadow of a memory.
I am grateful and filled with love
for all those who assisted in
shaping me into who I became.
I am the hope, joy, and experience
of all that was.
I am a free spirit.

—Jake

CONTENTS

ACKNOWLEDGMENTS

I wish to give a very special thanks to my husband, Les, who has given me wonderful support and joy during the time taken in writing this book. My friends, Pamela Way, Marie Douchkoff, Lisa Doran, Ann Marie Herlihy, Kristen Robinson, and Carol Noreika who gave me their very own individual loving support in getting this book published. To my twin brother, Gene Tuminelli, a very special thanks for his love, belief, and who has helped make this publication possible. A heartfelt thanks to Paul A. Elwell, DVM, who relentlessly and lovingly assisted us through all the many times of need. He was fantastic and I am so grateful to him even to this day.

In appreciation to my children, Dawn, Stacey, and Scott for their heartfelt love and care toward all of our pets.

PROLOGUE

The air always smells so fresh and clean. To be here in this place is forever so wonderful. The light that is here is ever so bright, delightful, cozy, and pleasant. How great it is to be forever. To never go hungry, to never feel sadness, loneliness, or pain. To be able to know and experience absolute love and joy. To play, to run, to jump, and to be happy never ends. What a wonderful place to be!

CHAPTER 1

Memories

Some time back, as my friends and I were running and playing, I stopped suddenly and thought I heard in the distance a familiar sound and sensed a familiar scent of long ago; memories began to take shape and flood my thoughts. I was beginning to feel forgotten emotions. Just then, somewhere in this place and time, something compelled me to search out more. As I moved forward, I told the others to go on without me. Soon I came upon a small grassy spot where the smells were mixed with heavier scents of things I had not thought about for a long time but were always deep within me. The sounds I could hear were fading in and out. These sounds and smells were in my memory from days of uncertainty and joy. But why are these things coming back to me here and now? I wondered if I needed to remember these things for a reason? Just maybe? Hmmmmm?

For sure, at this time, I am not nervous or scared in any way! Not in any way for it could never exist here. I am in a place of pure love and security. Yet my curiosity was certainly strong!

Since I decided to stay here for a while, I searched and scratched the grass to be sure that no other creature was going to lie down with me. Comfortably settled, I began to reflect on a lifetime long ago that wasn't so joyful and safe. For you see, in that lifetime, I was a dog. Even now, in this beautiful, happy, safe place, I am still a dog. With this in mind and moving forward, I find my memory takes me to a time of younger years and all that came to be.

As I recall, it was in the year of our Lord. Okay, I know! It's just that I always wanted to say this. I heard many stories that were read to others that started out like this. I really don't know what it means, but it sounds important. Anyway, in those days, I was somewhat oblivious too many things and, at times, a bit rough and untamable. Being happy and carefree wasn't always in my favor, you might say. There were times I thought all I needed was attention! Really, I'm not making this up! It took a while for me to understand that my way wasn't always a good way to get the attention I so wanted. Hmm, just maybe this is part of something I had to learn. Perhaps these memories will provide an answer to this.

You see, in that lifetime, I was a particular breed, known as a dalmatian. Now while in those days of happiness, and yes, also as a bit of a troublemaker, I was given the name Jake—a name that I was proud to have because of when and who gave it to me. But for now, let's just back up a bit and explain how I first received the name Jake. Wow, I am amazed at how all these memories are coming back to me as I ponder more.

There is one more thing before continuing. First of all, I cannot begin to express my heartfelt days of loneliness, hunger, being scared, and many times just not knowing where I'd find shelter or if I'd ever be loved. Oh sure, there was the joy of being my own boss, being dirty, smelly, and carefree. You know, doing whatever I wanted and whenever without restrictions. So much fun that was too! Hmm, yeah, like who was I really kidding? As I think on this for sure, it was myself. After all, I was a dog! A dog who was to be serving my human beings. What was that saying? Oh yeah! "Man's best friend." That's what I was supposed to be—man's best friend! Well, with all my carefree running, who was really there to care for me? But more importantly, who was I to care for, protect, and love? Just who?

Also, I sure did miss being hugged, petted, and getting those scratches. Oh, those scratches, especially on my back and down my chest. You know, the harder places for me to really get to easily. Wow! I really did miss that. Oh heck, the truth being, it was being scratched anywhere!

Okay, moving forward, prior to my carefree days, I was born with nine brothers and sisters in open land under some kind of shelter that Mom had found for protection. Wow, big family. Mom was smart and did the best she could with all of us. We were always hungry and trying to suckle her milk. It was good too. She was a good mom and made sure we all took turns so none of us would be left out. If one of us tried to get in to suckle her before the other was done, she would gently push us aside and explain to us about patience and taking turns so we would all have a better chance of survival. She told us many times that it was important we respected and looked out for one another. Mom was also a good hunter who kept herself strong and healthy. Pretty too! Although I must mention that I wasn't sure at those times why she taught us to stay hidden when she went out for her food.

One day, I noticed that we were all changing in size and the way we looked. We were developing spots. Most of us had these black spots while a couple of my sisters had brown spots and one brother had mixed colors. We were all changing and getting so big that staying inside this place was getting very crowded.

As time went on, we were also able to slowly stop drinking only Mother's milk and started eating the food she brought back for us. I don't know what the stuff was that she brought back, but I can remember it was good. With all of us growing so much, we needed to eat more and more.

So Mom began to let us go with her for short distances and watch how she would get us food. Got to admit, things were very different out there. There was so much to see and learn. How did Mom know what to do and where to go? The best part of being outside was that there was more room to run and play.

As we grew, our playing, at times, would be some light fighting with growling noises, light biting, pulling on one another's tail, and knocking one another to the ground. Playing was a very big part of our life. It was always fun, except the times when Mom would get a bit upset with one of us if we crashed into her too much. One thing for sure, we all loved each other. As a dog, being a bit rough with one another was also going to help us survive in case we needed to protect

15

ourselves as Mom would tell us. I didn't understand much about having to protect myself; after all, life was full of playing and running. My breed, especially, loved to run a lot.

Hmmm, just a minute, something just occurred to me. In recalling my memories, I realized I am able to relive every moment by moment like it was just happening but without the emotions of fear, sadness, or whatever I had experienced at that time. Interesting! These were only the memories that I am able to share without affecting me in any way at this time. It's as if it was another life and not quite my own. However, every detail very strongly remains with me.

Oh, before I continue, just give me a minute to get more comfortable. So a little standing, stretching, turning, sniffing the area, and checking just in case any little creature might have joined me. I wouldn't want to crush anyone. After all, we all exist here in peace and unity. Okay, this should do nicely. Now being nice and cozy again, I can settle back down and recall these memories.

CHAPTER 2

Unexpected Events

Drifting off to those times again, I remember that day all too well, which was the beginning of a new life for me. It was a very hot day with everything now drying after the water had come down from above throughout the darkness. More importantly, it was time for all of us to go out and play. What fun we were having! Mom told us to stay near one another. My one brother and I were playing chase. He couldn't catch me because I was a very fast runner, and I kept running farther and farther away from him. I loved to run! When I turned to find him, he was nowhere in sight. *Boy, am I fast, or did he just give up?* I thought. As I started back, I noticed a little creature scurrying along the ground. So being very curious to find out what it was and maybe it would play with me, I followed it for a long time till it went into a small hole in the ground and wouldn't come out again. Well, that wasn't much fun. I waited for it to come out again, but it never did. I was getting hungry and thirsty. It was getting late and time for me to get back to my family. I'm sure Mom was getting worried by now.

But, oh no, I realized, which way did I come from? "Okay, stay calm and remember what Mom taught you," I said to myself. I'd have to use my nose and follow my own scent back. All was going well until I saw a dark shape on the ground. Great! This was going to be a fun day. I had something else to play with. Even though I didn't know what it was, chasing it was going to be fun. Finally, I was able to pounce on it. But wait a minute, nothing happened, and I didn't feel anything under me. The dark thing moved out from under me so fast. What? How did that happen that I pounced on the ground, and it quickly moved right out from under me? The dark shape continued to move in circles and was getting bigger. Now I will pounce on you again, and this time, just then I happened to look up and saw this great big dark thing above with big wings coming toward me. It was much bigger than the ones I chased out of the bushes back home. Yet, this time, something didn't seem right to me. I sensed that I had better take cover, like Mom taught us. But where to go? Keeping low and running as fast as I could in all different directions was very important. My heart was beating faster and faster. I could now hear the sounds of the wind from its wings getting closer and closer to me. Then all of a sudden, I felt something on my back that caused me great pain. At this time, I became confused and so scared as I felt myself being lifted off the ground. *Oh no*, I thought, *what's happening to me!*

I yelled "Mom! Mom, help me! Help me!" I yelled over and over.

These things in my back were hurting me, and I knew that I just had to get loose before it was too late. As I was being lifted up and down, then back up a bit again, I growled, and wiggled. Giving it my all, I fought as hard as I could. This worked and it let go of me. I fell a bit hard (and grateful that it wasn't to high) onto the ground, rolled over onto my paws, got up, and ran as fast as I could to get away from it. I could see the circling of its darkness around me as I ran.

I panicked. It was coming at me again! This was something for sure that I didn't want to play with. My back started hurting me, and I was getting really tired. As hard as it was, my fear gave me strength to run faster than when I did with my brother earlier. But no, I thought *this cannot be happening*. Again, I called for Mom over and over and over, but she didn't answer. After all, she couldn't hear me. I was too far away. Oh, why didn't I listen when she said to stay close to home? Too late now. I am on my own. I didn't know where to go or what to do. Only that I just had to keep running and running. While I was thinking of Mom and running, I wasn't paying attention to what was happening until I felt another sharp pain on my back. Thinking fast now, I flipped over onto my back and rolled away. I escaped again as it flew up higher above me. This was getting very scary for me. My mind was panicking, but I had to keep thinking clearly, or I wasn't going to make it. Oh, Mom, where are you?

"Try to remember what you learned from Mom," I told myself.

Then just shortly up ahead, I saw some bushes. Hoping I could get in them, I ran even faster—just in the nick of time too! I dashed into the bushes as it came at me. This time, it made a loud long noise that hurt my ears. I quickly turned around. As I looked back and up, I saw it going higher and higher above me. Then something in the air caught my attention as it was falling to the ground from that awful big thing. Finally, after a short while, I couldn't see it anywhere. I hadn't realized how still and frozen in place I had become until moments later. It seemed to feel like forever before I even flinched a muscle. Then I realized that from all the heavy, fast running, it was hard for me to even breathe. Even though I was so exhausted, I began to wonder if it was safe for me to continue my journey for home, or would I be safe in here for now. What was that thing anyway? I'm sure when I get back home, Mom would explain everything. Then my scent got a whiff of what had fallen close to me on the ground from that thing. I realized that it must have been a part of its wing or so as it hit the bush just as I got into it. No sooner, to my relief, a strong wind came by and blew it away. *Good for me!* I thought. Having that reminder around was just horrible anyway!

Shortly afterward, I began to move a bit and realized that it was getting harder for me to see my surroundings, even the smells were different now. The air was cooler with a soft breeze coming into my so-called safe place. The light from above was now much dimmer. So being very exhausted, I decided it was best for me to stay hidden and rest. As I started to feel a bit more relaxed, I noticed that my breathing and my insides weren't beating as fast. In addition, another thing started to happen to me. There was some pain on my back, remembering now being picked up off the ground by that big black thing. Oh, it gives me the shivers just remembering! Even though it was hard for me to reach, I tried my best to lick that area and make myself feel better. At that moment, I surely did miss my mom's comforting ways and care, especially since I was so exhausted, hungry, thirsty, and still so very scared. At once, the loneliness overtook me. It caused me a sadness that came from so very deep within me that I began to cry for some time.

Finally, I told myself, "No! No more crying!" I didn't know if my crying was for missing home, my family, being angry at myself for getting in this predicament or relief that, for now, I was hopefully safe. Maybe it was a combination of all? Being all alone, I had no choice but to be strong and take care of myself. If I am going to make it, I have to be strong and think clearly!

As the darkness crept around my safe place and too exhausted to be scared still, I soon realized that leaving would have to wait for now. I was safe; water and food would have to wait till I felt better. Lying there in the quiet, licking my back area as best as I could, I began to understand the things Mom had taught us, especially play fighting, where she said that would come in handy in order to know how to protect ourselves. I guess she was right. If it wasn't for Mom, I just couldn't imagine where I would be at this very moment. You know, moms are amazing and seem to know a lot. Yet, once again, I did not listen, and she was right!

As I continued to lay still, I began to have pleasant thoughts of my family while trying to forget what had happened. Through my exhaustion and thoughts, I must have fallen off to sleep after all these unexpected events.

CHAPTER 3

Strange Happenings

Come the early brightness, I woke with the pleasant sounds of noises coming from small creatures. I could see that some were flying around, but nothing as big as what hurt me. Or, at least, that is what I was hoping. Then there were others scurrying around, looking for food or just checking things out. As I lay there watching, I was wondering if they would play with me or if I would find myself lifted again by that big black thing. I must be really careful which creatures I chase for play. Just then, I heard a different noise, and instinctively, I froze. *I really needed to get out of here and real fast too!* I thought. Then I realized the noise was not from outside, my safe place, but from around me. My thoughts became scrambled and I was scared that something was now in here with me that I didn't see before. Or could it be that that big thing somehow got in here without me noticing? Searching my area as I was able to, I could not find or smell anything other than just me in here. Yet this noise would not stop and was getting louder! Wait, wait, wait! I stopped and listened closely and realized, oh my! It was me! The noise was from inside of me. I was so very hungry and could not remember when I last ate! What a relief this was! I didn't understand for sure and seemed to feel a bit weird that these noises were from me; at the same time, I was truly very, very hungry and thirsty. I do remember that Mom was just starting to teach us how to hunt for our own food and what to be careful of. *I may have to apply those lessons now,* I thought. Yet I was so tired. Still, I have to move on.

After carefully checking my outside area and above, of course, I felt it was okay for me to venture out and start my way back home. However, as I tried to stand, things seemed a bit unsettling for me. I was feeling out of sorts. My head was light, my legs were shaking, and my insides were still making funny, loud noises. From all the past running, along with the pain on my back, I was beginning to feel other pains, and more things happening inside me. At that moment, all I could think about was getting home!

Peeking my head out of my safe place, I wasn't quite sure, at that moment, where my own scent was that would get me on the right trail back home. Eventually, I began to pick it up—for a while, at least. This made me very happy and excited. First, I went in a straight line for a while, then an area that was all messed up, back to a straight line, lost my scent, found it, then in circles again, went side to side, again in circles, and straight. Really! All this sniffing around and around, going straight, then around and again and again, all the time looking up and around in case that thing came toward me again was not making me feel any better. I had to be really careful about open areas and finding few safe places to take shelter. The brightness from above was making everything hotter and me even thirstier.

I had to stop for a while because my insides began to feel much worse than before. I must find shelter again. What? To my surprise, something was going on within my body. My nose was getting dry and cracked, as I was feeling very hot yet cold at the same time. I didn't have a clear understanding of what was going on but knew that it was not good, which, of course, was making me a bit nervous and not helping my situation. My body was beginning to shake, and all at the same time, my sides and chest started moving in and out while my mouth opened uncontrollably without me being able to stop it! What was going on? Something was trying to come up and out of my mouth from deep within me, yet nothing was really coming out. It was most uncomfortable and painful. When it finally stopped after a few minutes, I felt weaker and more tired than before. Honestly, I did not think I could feel any worse.

Where could I go to get some rest? Dragging myself as best as I could, I was able to see ahead a shaded bush area near some rocks, which seemed to be a good place to rest. All around me, the brightness was making the air heavier and harder for me to breathe. I was so very thirsty, weak, lonely, hungry, sad, and knowing all I really wanted was to just go *home*! I knew that I had to keep going and get my weakened body far away from other creatures. After what seemed like forever, I finally came upon the shaded bushy area. Being able to crawl in as best as I could, I dropped on the spot and hoped that I was hidden enough. As I was about to rest, my body started again being hot, cold, and shaking uncontrollably. Exhaustion was so overwhelming that soon I was beginning to feel myself going off into a deep, deep, much-needed sleep. If only I could understand all these strange happenings.

CHAPTER 4

New Encounters

Now mind you, I don't know how long I was there when something woke me. There were noises and strange smells, ones I never encountered before. I could barely open my eyes, let alone move my body. I felt so weak. Something was not right. Realizing there were strange creatures in front of me, I froze. What danger was I in now? How could I fight back, being so weak? Maybe I was dreaming? If it was not for the strong smells that came from these creatures, I was sure that this was not real. For a brief moment, my eyes opened again. I tried to see how big or what these creatures were. It was hard to tell since they kept moving in different directions in front of me. With the bright light and darkness coming between their movements, (later, I understood them to be shadows) it was difficult for me to know just how big these creatures really were. Honestly, at that time, it really didn't matter anyway. Once again, I felt so horribly scared. Not possible, but yes, even more scared than that thing that came at me from above! You see, before, I only had to deal with one creature. This time, there were a few of them. They seemed to be a whole lot bigger than that flying thing, and they also began to pull at me and tear away at my safe place. I was so weak and could not fight back. Now do you see why I was actually terrified?

In all my thoughts, *I could only think of was to just leave me alone!* I was in a safe place, and no one was to find me! All I needed was to rest and then find my way back home. With a low grunt, thinking it was very, very loud, I called for Mom. I needed her more than ever.

WHEN WE MEET AGAIN

"What do I do now, Mom? Mom, I need you!"

No response! The fact of the matter is these creatures wouldn't leave me alone. The smells and noises coming from them were extremely frightening to me, especially as I felt myself being dragged out, which made the pains in my back more excruciating than before. I really tried and wanted to fight them, yet all I could do was make a faint growling sound. That was the last thing I remember from that place.

Well, to my surprise, when I began to wake up, something was very different. I didn't remember what had happened to me or how I got to where I was. The first thing I noticed was that the smells were very unpleasant to my senses. Also, it was interesting that my body didn't feel as hungry, thirsty, or as painful as it was before. Then all at once, it came back to me! *Strange smells and those creatures pulling at me while I was in my safe place,* or so I thought, and me being so terrified. Anyway, I realized that I wasn't in the open anymore. How did I get here? Who and what were those strange creatures? Why was I feeling better and not worse off than before? What was going to happen to me? What did they want from me? Where was I? How will I get out and back home? What were these smells that were making me feel very nervous? As I searched my new surroundings, I didn't see those creatures anywhere. Again, how did I get here and why was I feeling better? Now don't get me wrong, it felt good to feel better! Also, how long was I in my safe place? My only thoughts were that wherever I am, when I get a chance, I'll make my run. I'm fast and I'll get away. In the meantime, I knew enough to stay very still, like Mom had taught us until it was safe to leave.

As I continued to lie there on my side, I started to see things, which, of course, I had no idea what they were. For sure, there weren't any kinds of bushes, rocks, or trees for me to get to. I seemed to be in a place that was higher off the ground. Oh, that just reminded me of being lifted off the ground by that flying thing. "Forget that for now," I told myself. Gotta be strong! When I do escape, where would I go? The brightness here was dull, and the air was so still with a strange, unfamiliar smell in the air. The ground I was lying on was hard, in some ways different yet kind of comfortable and relaxing.

25

It wasn't grassy or rocky as usual. Something was under me that was soft and comforting. Almost like the piles of ground we would put together before we slept but better. I thought it to be pleasant. Maybe this wasn't so bad after all. There also seemed to be something all around me. I was in a small confined area unlike the bushes I had been in. Even though I couldn't see anything above me, below me, or on either side, it felt a bit safe and even cozy, like my safe place before. In front of me, I could see out, yet there was some kind of thing that blocked my clear view that I could not understand. Being curious as I am, I reached out with one paw to see if it was real or not. Even though I could get a small part of my paw through it, something very hard and thin stopped me from going further. Now this was strange, and I didn't like it one bit. At that moment, it came to my attention that, for some reason, I was feeling stronger. With this new realization, *I could now take my chance to use both of my paws to break through and make my run for it,* I thought, especially since I hadn't seen any of those strange creatures. As I tried to move my other leg, to make my escape, something was keeping me from moving it as easily as my other one. What was happening now? There was some kind of attachment to my leg that went on the other side of this space that I was in! Something else was inside my leg as I noticed it was hidden by a thing that was wrapped around my leg at the same time. Not understanding or liking this one bit, I began to bite at this thing on my leg to free myself and get out of here fast.

Then it happened! Oh no! I heard those familiar noises and saw those strange creatures again. My insides began to shake. My heart began to pound more and more. I lost my chance to escape! What were these things anyway? There were two of them. As I watched them, I noticed that they were big and walking on their hind legs and for such a long time too! Then one of them started to come over to me. So I quickly closed my eyes and kept them closed. I could feel the breath on my head coming from this creature and felt my heart pound even more. The breath was warm, a bit heavy, and the smell was again unfamiliar and unpleasant to me. I had nowhere to go and thought this was it. How could I fight this big thing while my one leg was not able to move easily, and this thing I was in was so small.

This was definitely worse than that creature that tried to pick me up off the ground! At least I was able to have enough room to fight back and had a clear chance to run. So what was I to do now? I would have to do my best. *Here goes my fight*, I thought. Just then, I heard some kind of strange noise coming from this creature! So I decided to stay still to see if this thing blocking my escape would be gone.

As this creature continued to make this noise for a while, it seemed different and not so scary anymore. I began to relax a bit. Why, you ask? I don't know! It was just happening that way. Then something else happened! It was a surprise and startled me a great deal. Something touched me on my head. Oh, here it is now. I opened my eyes wide and quickly turned my head to bite it. After all, I had to protect myself in any way that I could. The creature moved its claw or whatever it was quickly out of my reach. *So they are fast, but the next time, I'll get you, and you won't hurt me,* I thought. It continued to make soft noises toward me and once again touched my head. I attempted to bite it again, but that quick move seemed to make me very tired and weak. Just maybe I wasn't as strong as I thought I was. All I could do was lay there, make growling noises, and hoping this would scare it away. But once again, it touched my head with soft scratching—something like I do to myself—only not as hard as I do to myself. To my surprise, I didn't turn to bite, especially since I felt so weak, and the scratching did feel kind of comforting and weird at the same time. *Wow, what was this all about?* I thought. The gentle scratching turned into some gentle rubbing on my head. It felt as though my mom was licking me, but it was not a lick, and there were soft noises still coming from this creature. Yet I didn't feel as scared as I had been. All this stuff seemed to exhaust me, and once again, I soon fell asleep. So many things coming at me all the time. Would I be able to survive with these new encounters?

CHAPTER 5

Close Encounters

Time moved forward. However long that was, I had no idea. I felt myself getting stronger and stronger. Also, I began to feel more comfortable around these two-legged, hind-walking creatures who seemed to take good care of me. There was always food, water, scratches, rubs, and some gentle, caring noises directed at me.

Best of all, while being in this confined area, they took off that thing that was attached to my leg, which now I know is called an IV, since I was feeling much better. And I really was! Now not knowing how long I was in there for, it came to be that one brightness, they opened the door, and I was able to get out on my own and walk around. It really felt good to get out of there. My legs, at first, did feel a bit weird, but soon I was walking and running around. I felt so happy! Then a new feeling had come over me. It was a good and safe feeling. Since I was able to walk on my own, they guided me to a different area where I could smell the open air and see high above me. This reminded me of that thing that had flown above me and hurt me. I had to stop thinking about that because I now feel safe and would not let that worry me anymore. However, I would always check above me. For now, there was a feeling of open ground under my paws again, a place to do my business and a sense of security.

Many times, these two-legged, hind-walking creatures would scratch and touch me. It had become quite comforting and soothing, which made me look forward to it. I was also able to know which two-legged creature would come toward me by the special smell they each carried and the specific noises coming from them. At first, there were just the two of them. Then more and more came toward me. I wasn't scared anymore and welcomed them.

Oh, oh, how could I have forgotten? Let me tell you this. There was that first time when one of the creatures picked me up. Yeah, could you imagine? It picked me right up. It reminded me of that thing above me and, at first, scared the life out of me, again! My memory also reflected quickly on how mom would carry us around when we were little by the back of our necks, but this creature did it differently. All of me came off the ground so unexpectedly that I thought I was going to be dropped. Instead, it held me so close it seemed as if it was going to crush me, though it never did happen. Lucky me! I wasn't sure what to do at that time, but something inside me sensed I would be okay. After being held so closely for a bit, it began to feel so wonderful that I accepted it. While being held like that, this particular creature continued to make soft noises, kept scratching and rubbing me at the same time. It was such an interesting experience for me and so unexpected. So anyway, that was my first time having this very close encounter with them.

Each creature that picked me up after that or spent time with me had different ways of interacting. Some made soft noises and would pet me very softly along with gentle scratching. Others would make loud noises and use their paws (which were their hands, I learned later) to turn me onto my back quickly to scratch my belly. Wow, that was the greatest feeling! Sometimes others would throw this thing that was called a ball for me to chase and bring back to them to only throw it again for me to bring back. This would go on for a while. I wasn't sure if this was something that they didn't want to keep for themselves, or it was just playing. Either way, for me, all these interesting experiences gave me such close encounters.

CHAPTER 6

New Realizations

In time, there were others that I was allowed to play with who were in other cages, as I also learned to be called. There were some who were like me yet different in ways. There were some tiny baby creatures that I almost wanted to eat for some reason but was told by these two-legged creatures to be gentle to them. Soon I understood what gentle meant. Being a quick learner, the two-legged creatures seemed to be pleased with me. These tiny creatures were called kittens whose mommy, for some reason, wasn't around any longer to care for them.

I understood how that felt, and my compassion turned toward giving much affection for these little guys. I began to stay with them more and kept them company. They would play and jump all over me. How much I truly loved it! This play reminded me of my family—whom I did miss very much. Yet I didn't seem to want to get home as fast, but I still wanted to get home—wherever that was now. But having these little guys to stay with was good for all of us.

Being interested and curious all the time, I noticed how these two-legged creatures took care of so many four-legged creatures. Some of them were sicker than me, and some were here for only a short while. These two-legged creatures seemed to really care, and at times, I could feel their sadness when someone they cared for didn't make it or would have to leave after being here for a while. I could also feel their joys and happiness. They truly did help give us four-legged creatures back our good health and happiness. I got to like this place.

Life here seemed to be going great until, one brightness, they put something around my neck. It felt strange and uncomfortable. I wanted it off and fought to get it off, but I could not get it off.

They kept speaking softly to me while gently petting me and saying, "Easy, boy. Easy, boy. It's going to be all right."

Yeah, keep telling yourself that. You put this thing around your neck and see what happens! I thought. I realized soon that I was still able to breathe with it on me, and it wasn't as tight as I was letting on to be. Soon they didn't seem to pay much attention to it, and yes, I did get used to it! Actually, when they did take it off, I did feel kind of free yet missed it. The so-called collar was becoming a part of me, and I felt kind of cool wearing it.

There seemed to be surprise after surprise for me. After having the collar on for a while, they attached a so-called leash to it. Well, with that leash attached to my collar, they began to pull at me. Didn't like that either. This was a bit confusing, uncomfortable, and made me scared at first. Once again, in time, I began to accept this and found it was not so bad. Actually, whenever they attached the leash to my collar, they would take me for walks.

I was also beginning to understand some of their noises and what they wanted from me. In a weird kind of way, they seemed a bit like my mom—always teaching me new things to do, and afterward, I would get some tasty treats. Mom taught us but never gave us tasty treats. Now mind you, because we didn't get treats, I'm not saying in any way that she wasn't appreciated or loved. She really taught us a lot. That is until I got lost, and now I don't know what else she would have taught me. Well, when I get back home, I hope she will teach me what I missed out on. Yet, being here, I am learning so much. This is great for me.

Then one brightness, to my surprise, somewhere in my memory, I remembered something that mom told us about two-legged, hind-walking creatures. These must be the ones she was telling us about. It had to be! She said that there were these two-legged, hind-walking creatures that were all around. Sometimes they would see her and try to catch her for some reason. She didn't know why, but something told her to not get caught. Others would chase her away

31

or maybe try to hurt her by throwing things at her. One time, she did get a little hurt by a hard thing that hit her on her back leg. Still, others would throw food to her and give her some water to drink. Sometimes the food that they threw at her she would bring back to us. She said that we should be careful, and like all creatures, some would be okay to play with. But for now, until we got bigger, she said to stay away from them. We had to use our best judgment. What that meant at the time was not clear. As I learned, these so-called two-legged, hind-walking creatures were called human beings or humans for short. Boy, if only she was here with me now! And this place, I learned, is called an animal hospital. And the people who found me in the hidden bushes were some who work here.

Being around these humans for some time now, I just didn't understand as to why mom was telling us that we needed to be careful around them. All they were doing for me was giving me food, shelter, playtime, learning new things, and we developed a warm feeling among us that I could sense. However, I just knew that I should heed what mom said; after all, she was Mom and had much more life experience than me. So I decided to keep my senses keen to every experience and appreciate my new realizations.

CHAPTER 7

Reflections

looking pretty good, right!

Time passed, and brightness turned into darkness and back again, over and over. I felt myself getting stronger and bigger. One time, when the humans left the door open, I began to explore other areas. I soon found myself in another place and noticed that there was another dog that I hadn't seen before. He must have just arrived. This made me very happy to have a new friend who seemed to look a lot like me. Yet seeing him reminded me of my family that I missed lately!

At times, when I cleaned myself, I noticed all my spots and markings, which seemed to look exactly like his. For sure, he's very strong, big, and a good-looking guy with very, very nice markings. I just couldn't wait to get closer to him and to sniff to see what he was all about. Also, it had to be clear to him that I would be the one in charge. After all, this is my territory, and I have to protect it as best I can. As I got closer, it seemed very unusual that I still hadn't picked up on his scent. Was there something wrong with me? Did he pose a threat to us? I just couldn't understand this strange experience as to why I couldn't get his scent even as we came closer and closer toward each other! Not good! Everything has a scent. So what's up with him? I began to wonder. As I continued to walk toward him, he also walked toward me. When I stopped, he stopped. What? It was kind of crazy and confusing to me at first, but we must have been a bit cautious of each other.

When I got very near to him, he stopped and stared into my eyes. *Very bold of him*, I thought. My head tilted, and so did his. My ears moved forward, and so did his! When I tried to sniff him, he still had no scent! Could you imagine that? No scent. Nothing! I even tried to check out his backside to be sure that we would be friends. But no matter how I tried to get around the back of him, he would disappear.

Then when I went face-to-face, again, he was there. Then I went again to sniff his backside, and again, he disappeared. This was so strange. Who or what would not have a scent? Well, this was a first. This time, I got real close and touched my nose to his nose, and all I felt was this cold hard thing. What was going on? When I reached out to touch this dog, my paw hit something hard. Okay, he must be playing with me. I had to be smarter. So I decided to trick him. I had to do a quick soft jump to see his reaction. But as I jumped, so did he, and still, I hit something hard.

As I stood tall on my hind legs, I noticed the bottom of his belly. Whoa, it looked rather familiar to me! Is this one of my brothers on the other side of this thing and we cannot touch or smell each other?

My instincts told me that somehow I would have to get him out of this thing and save him. But how? I got down, and after a while of this nonsense, I noticed that in this hard thing, I also saw other things that were in this room that showed as well. Things behind me were in it too! How could this be possible? Something was very, very suspicious. As I turned around further, I noticed other things in this room that had the same dog as me. Where were they coming from and why?

Just as I was beginning to get a bit freaked out, a human came into this room and said to me, "Oh, I found you, handsome." She noticed that I was a bit uncomfortable and said, "I see you found yourself looking in these shining things. These, big guy, are called mirrors. Must have been real funny and confusing for you at first." She chuckled a bit and gently patted me on my head and back. This human was called Meg, who then told me, "To take it easy, big guy, it's only your reflection in these mirrors."

Oh? A mirror! This made me feel better. I learned another human word along with having another interesting experience. Wow! Would things ever stop, or would my life be full of many, many more experiences to come? Anyway, I still thought that the so-called reflection in the mirror was good-looking. If that was what I looked like, then pretty good. Yep, pretty good! Mom would be proud of me if she could only see my reflections.

CHAPTER 8

Alone Again

Every now and then, I would find myself back in the room with the reflections or mirrors and could see how much bigger I was getting. My thoughts wondered, I didn't know how long I was here, but life was good, and I was feeling really happy these days. I was also going outside more to meet others similar to myself. We would sniff, play, and run around together. The humans took me for more walks on the leash, and I was having a great time being here with them.

I had also become very close to this one human called Jackie. She always brushed me, gave me lots of hugs, and attention. Jackie would talk to me a lot. I was really understanding her words, and she would read books and the letters she received from her boyfriend, Greg, to me. I understood Greg to be somewhere far away. She mentioned the word war a few times. This was something I seemed to have trouble comprehending. Yet I knew it was not very nice. She would become very sad in certain parts of her reading, and sometimes water would come out of her eyes. That would make me sad as well. So, I would get really close and lay my head on her lap. Sometimes I would look up and give her a nice lick. Especially when the water came from her eyes, I would lick them away. This would somehow make her laugh and happy again.

Jackie would tell me over and over what a good boy I am and how much she loved me. Love—now that was an interesting and powerful word. Whenever she would say this to me, how much she loved me, I could sense something from within her, and especially around her chest area, a big energy change. Her chest area, especially, would send off such a glow of brightness in addition to mine, feeling an immense surge of deep affection, warmth, kindness, and joy. So I guess this is what love is about. It sure is a great emotion! The times we spent together were great, and I always looked forward to them. I missed her when she wasn't with me.

Then one brightness, when Jackie came to see me, something was very different. There was a real deep sadness that surrounded her, and it concerned me very much. She started to tell me that she wasn't coming back for a long time. What? No, you cannot go! She was my best friend, and I needed her as much as she needed me! Then she said something about Greg not ever coming back to her again. She then had lots of water coming from her eyes, more than I had ever seen before. Even when I licked them away and tried to jump on her to play with, Jackie wouldn't stop with the water and just hugged me. She wouldn't let go! Her chest area was in such pain, and sadness was all over her. It was so very, very deep with pain. I could feel it myself. All I could do is hug her back. After some time, she let me go and then said goodbye to me. I started to whimper, and my sadness got deeper. She said to be a good boy and that she loved me very much but had to go away. She also said that she hoped I find myself a wonderful home someday soon. I deserve it. This part really confused me. What did she mean find a wonderful home? This is my home. Then she hugged me again and left as she said how much she did really love me.

I stood there for a moment then started to run after her. Meg came over and stopped me. She told me everything would be okay and to let Jackie go. At that point, I felt so alone, again!

CHAPTER 9

Mixed Emotions

As I was getting older and stronger, I began to take notice, or I should say I was becoming more aware of things. Like my nose was becoming more sensitive, my sight keener, and my hearing sharper. I could sense more awareness within me. I didn't know why; it just was.

Even though I had Meg and the others, I still missed Jackie. There were a lot of distractions during this time because I noticed that more and more strange humans came to pet, play, and talk to me. Then I wouldn't see them again, except this one time when this family came back. Since my senses were becoming more skilled, I remembered their scent from before, and I had mixed emotions about them, especially the leader of the pack who was a very big human. Even though he smiled and laughed a lot, he seemed a bit scary to me at times. His scent was stranger and somewhat slightly unpleasant than the others in his pack—a scent that I hadn't encountered from any human so far. It's like he was hiding something. I just wasn't sure what it was about him, yet! Then there was the big female, who must have been his mate. She had a softer, pleasant scent about her. Although there was a hidden sadness that was below the smiles and laughter, I could trust her and liked her. The little pup or human male was small and a bit taller than me. I could just about look at him eye to eye. He was very playful and a bit rough with me at times. I think this was his way of playing. He would pull on my tail that hurt sometimes and then laugh when I jumped around to free myself. He did laugh a lot and was very playful. The female would tell him to be nice and go easy. I was sure she was his mother, one like mine that I haven't seen in a long while.

I wondered why they came back to play longer and took such an interest in me this time. Then they took me outside in the big yard where we had fun chasing each other. The little pup was fun to play with in a different kind of way too. When he fell on the ground, I would jump on him and lick his face. He had a very cute laugh, which encouraged me to play and lick him more. When I wasn't licking him, he would grab my tail, which was getting kind of sore. His mom would chase him a bit to have him stop pulling on my tail so much. It was one big chase after another. Who was chasing whom? We all seemed to be having lots of fun, though.

After we went back inside, the energy changed. Things became a bit serious. I was left alone for a bit, and when they came back Meg put the leash on me again. Oh good, I get to go for another walk. But before I left for a walk, some of my human friends that took care of me came over and started petting and hugging me while saying things like, "Nice knowing you, big guy" or "Take it easy and be good." Why did I have to be good? Wasn't I already good? Now why would they be saying these things to me? Then bang! Wham! It hit me. Oh no! Whenever I heard those words before, I never got to see my other four-legged friends again. *Did that mean that I would be going away too? Where would I be going? This was my home,* I thought. My first home with humans who took care of me, fed me, played with me, and loved me. I don't understand! Is this what Jackie was talking about before she left too? Is this how it happens? Didn't I have anything to say about it? How do I handle this? I'm getting such mixed emotions!

CHAPTER 10

Away We Go

Soon I was being led out with this family. Again, I began to wonder what was happening and why was I going with them and not my other human friends. Was I being taken away from this place because I was bad? I felt sadness as I saw some water coming from the eyes of some of my human friends who stayed behind and looked at me with a heavy heart. Yet this family that I was going with seemed happy. A lot of mixed emotions and energy was coming at me all at once.

Plus, why wasn't I able to see my four-legged friends to say something to them before I got taken away?

Once outside, we went toward one of these strange things that had wheels, called trucks and cars, as I learned. Somewhere in my faint memory, I remember being in something like this. Oh, that was just before I arrived here when I was so sick. Yeah, that's when I was in one. Just don't remember too much of it. Though I do remember that when my other human friends took me for walks, I would see these things move very, very fast past us, and they could be a bit scary. The really big ones, especially, were scary and seemed dangerous if you weren't careful. The ground would shake under my feet way before they even got near us. Then when they went past us, I could feel the strong wind. The loud sound of noise that came from it was almost too much for my ears, and the stuff that blew up at us from the ground, as they went by so fast, was messy. All these car and truck things that moved seemed so powerful.

We seemed to be heading right for a particular one, and the leader, the daddy, as the small pup would call him, had something in his hand that he put into a small hole in the side of the car. It made a deep click noise as he turned his hand and then opened it up. Before I realized what was happening, because I was interested in all the things around me as well, the leader lifted me off the ground quickly and put me into a cage of some kind in a small area inside this car. I could see from side to side, but not above or below me. While I was sniffing and checking things out, I heard a slam that kind of startled me. As I looked out, everyone else didn't seem to mind, so I felt okay. At first, I thought they were going to leave me in here by myself, and then I saw them open doors, bent down to only sit down, and put things around them. It must have been their leashes. Hmm, didn't know humans wore leashes. Guess we have some things in common after all. The smaller pup, who was called Phillip, sat near me and seemed to be very excited while laughing a lot. He was trying to touch me through the cage. The daddy, called Joe, and the mommy, called June, both seemed to have two names. Phillip called them Daddy and Mommy. While Mommy called him Daddy or Joe sometimes, and Daddy called her Mommy or June sometimes. So I guess I can also call them either name.

Anyway, they each turned and said directly to me, "Okay, big guy, to your new home we go!"

Oh? I thought. Then I heard a strange noise of combined sounds. I immediately felt something jerk my body, and a weird movement started to occur. I had to catch my balance and change my stance so I wouldn't fall. Even though my legs and feet were still, things were moving faster and faster away from me as well as around me. This was an experience I wasn't sure of. As we moved farther and farther away from my friends, I could see them getting smaller and smaller. So this was it—me and my new family? Just like that, away we go?

CHAPTER 11

New Surroundings

As we continued to travel for some time, my attention went toward the different things that I began to see outside the cage and through the windows of this so-called car. Where could we be going? Things outside were changing for sure. There seemed to be fewer trees and hardly any grass, if any, which made me glad that I wasn't out there; also, where would I do my pee and poo without having grass or trees? After all, how could the others of my kind know where I would be marking my territory? Speaking of that, I hoped we would stop soon, or I would be marking this car.

Anyway, continuing my observations, I noticed there were more of these cars in different shapes and sizes and the really big ones that are scary to be near. The smells were different too, with more humans walking, some four-legged creatures similar to me were being walked as well. I saw one of them do his pee and poo right there on a really big sidewall. Really! By the way, these sidewalls were higher than I could see from my cage, and they were getting bigger and closer to each other. I thought, how sad that those four-legged creatures didn't have any trees or grass to mark their territory. Or maybe these really big sidewalls are just different kinds of trees. After all, I had never seen so many of these sidewalls so close together. Then there was the noise that seemed to be almost nonstop and louder. So busy! I hoped that we would not be staying in a place like this. I could not see any open spaces for me to run and play.

Turning my attention back to the others, I noticed there seemed to be a lot of excitement going on. They were talking to me, but I could not understand much at first since they were all saying things so fast and a lot at the same time. My other human friends would talk to me one on one and much slower. These humans were saying words I understood like "Good boy," "It's okay." Why were they telling me it's okay? Was something not okay? Was I to be afraid of something that might happen? My stomach was beginning to feel a bit weird from this long movement. This was reminding me of the first time my stomach was making those weird noises before I was put in a cage like this when I first woke up and all those things were attached to me. Even though it was for my own good, this experience was weirder. These humans seemed to be okay. They were laughing, talking, and looking at me a lot. It took a bit before I began to feel somewhat better and started to like this new movement. I guess this is what a car ride is from what I heard them saying.

These places we were passing were so busy, and each time the car stopped, I thought we were going to get out so I could do my markings. Yet no one was getting out, and the stop was only for a very short while, which seemed to take place many times. During these times that we stopped the car, many of these humans would walk in front from both sides. Wow, how many humans are there anyway? They seem like those little things that come out of the ground and crawl all over you so fast and sometimes bite. Oh yeah, I think they are called ants. I never know how many or where these ants are going to pop out of, just like the humans, I guess!

Oh good, finally, we came to a stop, and Joe, or Daddy, pulled over and got out of the car.

Then June, or Mommy, and Phillip got out too. Phillip was so excited that he was jumping up and down, and mommy had to calm him down. Boy, he's a funny human! When Mommy June got the leash, I knew that I was going to go with them for sure. I started to get excited and was jumping around as well in my little area. Hmm! Maybe Phillip and I are more alike than I think. So happy to get out because I sure couldn't wait another minute!

As I was getting out and sniffed more, I could tell that it was surely different from my other home.

The smells seemed to be heavier, and many, many were mixed together. It was kind of hard to tell them apart. Hopefully, I wouldn't have to stay here too long to know the difference. Anyway, it felt good to be out of the cage and car. There were no bushes or trees for me to do my marking and relieve myself. Gotta go so badly! There were so many buildings, big and small, as I learned them to be called. As I got closer to the strong scents, I found a particular one from another dog, and for some reason, I just lifted my leg then marked over it. That was a surprise to me and a relief to be able to go. Now my scent was stronger than the one that was just there. For some unknown reason to me, it felt good to be able to do that.

As I continued my walking and looking around, this place seemed to be more crowded with cars lined in rows while others in the middle were moving, some faster and some slower. There were many shaped buildings with some having yards, and others, none at all. I was led by Mommy June toward one that had a small play area and was fenced in. This also had a few stairs to climb. I like that feeling of climbing. It felt good to climb something instead of just walking straight all the time. Daddy Joe stayed behind and was taking things out of the car. As usual, Phillip was still jumping around and kept calling out a word or name of some sort while petting me and jumping in front of me a lot. It was Spirit. That's what he kept saying to me—Spirit. I think that was my new name.

Once we all went inside, there was much to take in—again, with all the different smells and many new rooms for me to explore. Mommy June led me around the different rooms, and I understood her saying that this room would be the one I would be staying in mostly. It was not too big and was separated a bit from the other areas of this new home. She removed my leash and allowed me to move around while she put some kind of barrier at the doorway. Great, another blockage to keep me from going out further as I had wanted to! I guess, for now, I would just check things out from here. Soon they brought me some water and food. I sure was hungry and thirsty. The food seemed to be the same as I had gotten before. Daddy Joe and Mommy June would come over to me constantly and talk to me. He sometimes would pat me on the head a little harder than I thought was necessary for me to enjoy. Mommy June would have to tell him to be gentle. Her touch was very loving and caring. I could see the love in her eyes, sadness, concern, and hope. She expressed many emotions at the same time that I could sense. I wondered why?

Mommy June would come and check in on me a few times. She and Phillip would take me out so I could do my business while checking out the neighborhood and getting to know what was going on. My sniffing around can tell me a lot of things, like who was here and if they were a bully, who seemed to own this area, who was a male or a female, the kind of humans hanging around, and so much more. So much to learn from sniffing. Some scents are stronger than others, and some not very pleasant either. But a scent is a scent with lots of information! Oh well, I guess new experiences go hand in hand with new surroundings.

CHAPTER 12

First Darkness

When darkness came, I was left alone in this smaller room by myself while they went to their rooms. I wanted to explore more of my new surroundings, but the barrier was strong and blocked me in. I felt like I was back in a cage, but this was bigger for me. My first time of darkness there was kind of lonely, and I was a little curious as to what things were in each room I could play with. It didn't have a nice energy to it for me. But I did like Phillip and Mommy June a lot. Daddy Joe was still a mystery to me.

You see, during the darkness time, I heard some loud noises coming from Daddy Joe and quieter ones coming from Mommy June but still loud enough to wonder what was going on. There seemed to be some not so nice things going on between the two of them. When Phillip went to check in on them, I heard really loud noises coming from Daddy Joe as I watched Phillip run back to his room with Mommy June following him. He seemed to be making similar sounds that Jackie made when the water was coming from her eyes. Was he all right? I wondered. Did he get hurt? I may have to look after that little one and Mommy June too!

Again, there was something about Daddy Joe that I just wasn't sure about. Mommy June seemed to be running back and forth between the two rooms, and at times, there were some very loud noises and banging sounds. I could feel vibrations through my paws and body. Not long after, it finally stopped, and things got quieter throughout the darkness. What could have been going on with everyone?

I had no way of understanding, so I just kept to myself. Of course, I had no choice. No one was paying any attention to me at this time. I began to remember the nice time that Phillip and I had earlier before all this stuff came about. Phillip was so happy to stay with me for a while, and we had some fun playing and lying down together on the bed, as he called it, that was on the floor.

He was petting me and talking to me, saying all kinds of things like, "I am so happy to have you," "You are going to be my pal," and "I love you" while he was scratching my head and belly. It was very comforting to me. I sure wished he was there with me then. I began to wonder if I would be alone like this from now on. At least at my other home, I had company from the others like my kind. I had to admit that it was a very long brightness and an exhausting one for sure—being taken away from my home, not knowing where I was going, seeing all the strange places, and wow, all the new smells.

Oh, also, trying to find a tree or bush, without success, of course, and then finding myself doing my markings on a wall, I believe, it is called. Then listening to Mommy June, Daddy Joe, and Phillip with the water coming down from his eyes. Things are so intense around here, and so was the whole experience from leaving and getting here. My instincts knew I still had to keep a cautious ear and be ready for anything around here. This bed that I slept on was pretty comfortable and very inviting. Maybe it won't be so bad living here. After much time of trying to stay awake, I got to sleep in my new home and made it through my first darkness.

CHAPTER 13

Protector

I woke up feeling very refreshed as my senses detected some very pleasant smells. I slept so soundly, which told me that I must have been more tired than I thought. So much for my cautious ear!

Very soon, Phillip came running over to me and pulled the blockage away so I could get out and play. My playing and jumping caused me to do some mess on the floor before I was taken outside. I hadn't any place else to go! When Daddy Joe saw this, he made a very loud noise at me, and then I felt a pain on my backside. What the heck was that? It hurt me, and I was so surprised, stunned, and scared that I ran to my soft place. He came over and grabbed my leash, put it on me rather hard, and then Mommy June came over quickly and spoke to him gently. She then took the leash with me attached, and we headed outside. I wasn't sure what happened, but I thought maybe my marking mess inside was not acceptable. Mommy June kept talking to me softly and rubbing my spot that still felt some sting. She was a nice human. When we went back in, Daddy Joe seemed a bit uneasy and gave me a mean look. Oh boy, I need to be careful around him. He carried a special and unpleasant odor, which has a very distinct scent, but at the time, I didn't know what it was. So my first time of new light or a good morning (as I remember my other human friends referring to as the new light came in) was not a very good start with my new family. Hopefully, I can do better, and maybe Daddy Joe will not be so rough with me.

As the good mornings and the darkness—the good nights—came and went, I became very fond of Mommy June and Phillip. I tried to keep my distance from Daddy Joe, though. Whenever he went to a special place in the cabinet and took out some bottle that had water in it, I guess, it made him very mean toward all of us. The scent that he carries seems to be much stronger after he drinks that special water from that particular bottle. This was the same scent I first picked up on him when we first met, only stronger after he drinks from that special bottle. I finally understood that this is where it was coming from! What could this have been and why would a human want to drink this stuff if it made him so mean? Mommy June and Phillip didn't drink from this bottle, and they didn't have that special scent that he did or were even mean like him. I drank my water and had no problem. So this must be a special water that is just for him. Hmmm!

The times that he drank that stuff, which seemed to be a lot, he would try to hurt me. Then Mommy June would try to stop him, and he would push her away. He was a big human, and I wasn't fond of him not being nice to us. Boy, that special water sure did make him mean. I noticed one time that Mommy June took some of his special water and poured some out. I don't know where it went, but there was much less in it that I could see. When she heard him coming, she quickly put it back. That was smart and kind of funny because when he took it out, he got this funny look on his face as he was looking at the bottle and then at her. She wouldn't look at him and just kept busy doing what she was doing. Humans are funny at times!

There was this one time when he was very mean to Phillip. Being that I was getting bigger and stronger, I found myself making a really big growl noise at him. He turned to me and yelled at me to "be quiet!" He proceeded to grab Phillip by the arm. I immediately found myself running in between the two of them, and I think I showed my teeth! I didn't know I was going to do that. Daddy Joe was hurting Phillip, and he had so much water coming from his eyes. Since Mommy June wasn't there, I had to protect him. When I got between the two of them, Daddy Joe got even meaner and started to take it out on me. He grabbed my collar and started to toss me around. Yes, this was scary and difficult for me to get my balance. I began to bark and growl really loud. When I tried to protect myself with a bite toward him, he dragged and kind of tossed me into my blocked off area and then threw the empty bottle at me. It missed, thank goodness. My chest was breathing in and out as I tried to get back out. My sad little Phillip tried to hide, but Daddy Joe pushed the table away and grabbed him again. This time, I got enough courage and strength that I leaped over the blockage and jumped on Daddy Joe's back. This surprised him as my forceful jump took him off guard, which made him fall. He moaned and stayed there for a bit. Mommy June quickly came in looked around at everything going on. She came to me first and took me back to my enclosed area where she took a little time to calm me down. Phillip was still crying and screaming. She ran over to Phillip, talked to him, picked him up, and carried him to his room. When she came back and attended to Daddy Joe, I heard her ask if he was okay? Then she told him that he tripped and fell. He looked over in my direction with a confused expression on his face. Shortly afterward, he got up and stumbled off to his room swinging his arms around and saying things that I could not understand.

Boy, that was close and scary. Maybe having a collar isn't always so great. I decided to stay where I was and be still for a while. All seemed to be quiet finally. As I lay still, I wondered why would humans want to live like this all the time instead of having fun, enjoying themselves with their family like I used to and just love one another? Mom did tell us that some humans were mean. Could mom have gone through the same thing or something like this? I sure hope she didn't have to experience what I did and she is okay. It has been so long since I had seen her, my brothers, and sisters. Would they even remember me? Even now, after all this time, I sure do miss them. Yet, for now, I knew that I had to be here as Mommy June and Phillip's protector.

CHAPTER 14

Just How

Many more good mornings and good nights came and went. When Daddy Joe wasn't around, we all seemed to be happy and having fun. There were long walks and times in a big park area where I could run and play with others like myself. I enjoyed those times very much. Sometimes when Daddy Joe wasn't drinking from that special water bottle that made him mean, he would take all of us out for a ride. So many things to see and experience! Daddy Joe would even spend time with me, throwing the ball and scratching my back. It did feel good. He was so nice and gentle when he wasn't drinking that special water.

Another time, as the good night was just starting to come, Mommy June and me were just getting back home when we heard Daddy Joe yelling at Phillip. We walked in seeing Daddy Joe hitting Phillip wherever he could. I immediately pulled away from Mommy June and attacked Daddy Joe. Everyone was screaming as I was pulling Daddy Joe away from Phillip by biting his pant leg and part of his leg as well. He turned and hit me across my head. I didn't expect that! It was a hard hit, and it hurt, but I would not stop protecting Phillip. Mommy June was trying to calm us all down. At that point, Daddy Joe turned and pushed her to the ground, grabbed me again by the collar, and dragged me out the door. I thought I was going to get choked, break my leg, or something! He dragged me outside and pulled me toward the car, opened the back, picked me up by the collar and under my belly while pushing me into the crate with such meanness. I was taken by surprise but was still ready to fight him. Outside the car, I noticed other humans were watching us with wide eyes and faces that looked so motionless. They seemed to be frozen in place. Daddy Joe was still yelling at me with words that were not clear. Everything happened so fast as he got into the car and took off with such force. The ride was so uncomfortable unlike the fun rides before. At that point, I was being tossed from side to side due to his driving. I just could not get my balance, and lying down wasn't any better! All I could do was stretch out and lean against the crate wall. I wasn't sure what was happening, but by this time, I was not feeling well. The car ride seemed to be forever when I realized that the darkness was upon us. Besides, I couldn't see much of where we were going anymore, though there were fewer and fewer buildings and hardly any brightness from other cars that I could see coming at us or even behind us. This was for sure the longest ride I had been on. I wondered where we were going and what we would do. From all that had gone on and how mean Daddy Joe was he was still saying things that were not clearly coming out of his mouth. Although, it did seem nice of him to take me for a ride!

Sometime later, we stopped. Where could we be? I didn't recognize any of these smells. The air was very refreshing and gave me a quick reminder of the open areas I used to play in as a young pup. Everything was so dark, except for the lights coming from our car and some light thing that Daddy Joe was holding on to. It was good timing that we stopped! I sure was ready for my markings and was careful not to do anything in the car, like I had done back home one time. Also, I was still feeling a bit uneasy from all the tossing back and forth during the ride. To my surprise, there seemed to be another kind of uneasiness that began to stir within me. A different kind of uneasiness, that is, like something I was sensing but didn't know what yet.

Throughout the car ride, as previously noted, Daddy Joe once in a while was saying things to me that didn't make any sense. At least I think they were to me since no one else was here but him and me! His words were hard to understand. Also, it took him a few minutes to get out of the car. As he was coming my way, he fell against the car then began to yell louder. Still, I couldn't understand his words. He quickly got himself standing up again even when his walking seemed unsteady. I saw him hit the car and wasn't sure why he did that. After all, I really didn't see anything that the car did to him that he should have to hit it! For sure, I was watching everything going on! As he walked over to me and opened the back door, then my crate, I didn't know what to expect from him. *Should I be afraid, on guard, defensive, or what?* I thought. He proceeded to pick up the leash, which was next to my crate, and put it on me. He pulled me out of the crate, but not as rough as when he had put me into it, which was a good thing!

I tried to be a good boy for him and hoped he would be nice to me. This place where we were was very different from any I had ever been to. So where were we? The air was definitely cleaner and had a crisp, refreshing scent to it. It was almost like the air I knew at the time being with my family. It was very dark here, and I could only see things clearly from our car lights. My senses became stronger, and I could hear things in the distance that became very quiet as we moved around more. It was like everyone out there didn't want us to know they were there, so they became very still. Smart of them too! Daddy Joe walked with me rather quickly off the road some and uneasily pulled me toward a small tree.

Great, finally, a tree! *Yes*! I could do my marking now like the old times! Yeah, this was not so bad going for a car ride. While I was busy doing my sniffing and markings, Daddy Joe was doing something with the leash and the tree. I was busy doing my marking again when I heard the sound of the car. As I looked up, I saw the car leaving. What? I tried to go but was stuck to the tree by the leash. Where was he going? I barked and pulled but was not able to get away from the tree. "Come back!" I barked again and again. "You forgot me!" I barked. I barked for so long that my bark sounded different. I jumped up and down and tried to pull away. He was so far away. Then I knew he really wasn't coming back! How could he do this to me, to Mommy June, and mostly, to pup, Phillip? Just how?

CHAPTER 15

What Do I Do

As I stood there confused, I could see the brightness of the car getting farther and farther away. Standing there for a few minutes, I thought and hoped he was going to come back. After all, that was my home, and I was a protector for Philip. Time went by, and I looked for the brightness of the car, but it wasn't there. Finally, I saw the light of the car. Well, I began to feel better that he was finally coming back for me. It was getting very scary out here and so very dark, except for the light that was way, way above me coming from that giant ball thing that I couldn't reach. It was really big, anyway, I probably couldn't fit it in my mouth. Yeah, he was getting very close, yet he didn't seem to be getting ready to stop. He was going so fast still and went right by me!

"Hey!" I barked. "You went past me! I'm here!" I barked again. "I'm right here! Turn around!" I barked. "I'mmmmmm heeeerrrre!" I barked, barked, and barked. He just kept going right past me and didn't even try to stop or slow down! Then I realized that it wasn't my car or Daddy Joe after all! Oh no! Please come back, please! At this point, even if it wasn't Daddy Joe, I would take anyone who would take me out of here. I watched it go farther and farther away from me as my insides felt so sad and shaky. For some time, I just stood there in disbelief, guess you can call it shock?

It took sometime for me to regain my wits, which made me realize I was going to be on my own—again! So now I had to figure out a way of getting out of here. I am stuck to this tree with little room to move. The darkness is great, I have no water, food, and only this little protection from this little tree. The sounds around me are ones that I am not use to hearing, at least not since long ago, which scared me then too! But mom was there to protect me and my siblings. Then I had this great idea! I would wait for another car to come by, jump out some, up and down, for it to see me. Surely, it would have to stop then and take me back home. But where exactly that is, I had no idea. After all, it was hopefully being with someone and better than here. So I waited, and waited, and waited for another car, only to find that there wasn't any! Gosh, where was I!

As I tried to get comfortable on this hard ground, I thought about how I am not used to staying out in places like this anymore. I missed my warm bed in its cozy corner, food, and water always being there for me. I was so afraid as I waited and waited for such a very long time. It was so dark, scary, and I felt so alone. Was anyone ever coming back for me? Do you think that Daddy Joe really meant to leave me here? Was he that mean to do this to me? Are Phillip and Mommy June okay? You know, she took a hard fall. Not only am I worried about them, but I have to get myself free from here. I must pay attention to myself at this point. Then I can concentrate on them. Agreed? Okay, agreed!

I tried to pull away with all my might; tossed, jumped around to free myself, tried to bite the leash, and still nothing. This was not as easy as I first thought, but I just couldn't give up! Then something amazing happened. As I backed myself away from the tree, I put my head down more and moved in a certain way that made my collar slip off my neck! Wow, a sense of great joy came over me! I was finally free after all the struggling and biting. Soon after, as I settled down, I had to figure out how to get back to Phillip and Mommy June. It was so very dark. Is it best to stay in one place for a little bit, or should I just start out and try to catch up? Besides, I was not sure which way was which yet. What do I do?

CHAPTER 16

What Happened After That

With the brightness of that big ball way up there, it was giving me guidance to get back home. I sensed I had to head toward the direction that Daddy Joe went. Right! Makes sense even if I am not able to pick up his actual scent. But I could still pick up the scent of Daddy Joe's car. Maybe if I run fast enough, I could catch up to him. Better run fast! During this time of running, I recalled my past of when I was in a similar situation, which made me sense what not to do and what to do this time around. By staying close to this area where the cars were moving, I could get back faster to my family. Being more aware this time around, if any creature came my way, I would not be so easily distracted in playing. Also, it never left me to always keep my awareness high in case anything flying from above comes at me. That is something I will always carry with me.

Except for the bright light coming from that very, very big ball way above, it was still very dark, which by the way, if only I could get to that ball, I bet it would be so much fun to play with! I just could never understand how that ball stayed in one place all the time and how did it get there?

I wonder! That time that Jackie threw the ball up and we never did find it, could this be the same ball? But this one is sooo much bigger! Yet why couldn't I get to it? I tried one time to jump as high as I could to catch it, but it is always too high up for me to bite on it. So I finally stopped trying. On my way now, once in a while, the ball light from above would go away then come back again. Was someone trying to play with me by hiding that ball? Oh well, I can't play now anyway. So I had better pay attention to what I am doing and where I am going!

In the distance, I could hear some noise and see a bright, very fast light coming from above in the area that I was heading. Not sure what it was all about, but something inside me said it was not good. I learned to listen to my senses and instincts. The air was beginning to smell different too, and the wind was beginning to pick up. Even though my running was keeping me warm, I could feel myself getting colder. The running on this ground was rough on my legs and paws. So with things being as they were, I had to be very careful not to get hurt. In order to get back faster and noticing the changes coming from above, I began to run even faster. It seemed to be taking such a long time to get anywhere! Then again, the ride was very, very long with Daddy Joe. So where could I have been and where am I going?

Throughout my time moving, there was only one car that came from the direction I was heading. As it got closer, the lights were very bright, which made it difficult to look at them. However, as I looked away, the brightness did give me better sight of what was around me. What I was able to see was not much. The land was dry and the bushes were very low. There didn't seem to be any shelter nearby, which I would be needing sometime soon by the smells in the air, the loud scary noises, and lights flashing from above were brewing up, as I could sense the sounds from above were coming closer, getting louder and longer.

As the car came closer, it was not slowing down. It just drove right past me very, very fast! I was smart to stay off to the side just like I did when Mommy June would walk me. Those things were scary and could be very bad if it touched me. I remember seeing a cat touch one of them. He yelled and then lay down very still and never got up anymore. Mommy June ran over to it and tried to help. I saw the cat look at me with a different look then close his eyes. After a moment or so, I saw him getting up in a very soft light kind of way. He looked at me again but continued to go up higher and higher till he was gone. He seemed okay. Where did he go? Weird, because he was still lying on the ground in front of us. *That was interesting,*

I thought. Soon, the one of him that was still lying on the ground began to smell different. Couldn't the humans smell the difference and did they see what happened as he went up and up then went somewhere? I watched as Mommy June picked up the one that was still there and wrapped him so lovingly in the paper she was carrying. She carried him home with us, and I never did see what happened after that.

CHAPTER 17

Round and Round

After some time of running, in the far distance, there were some lights. I decided to head that way since it was getting darker for longer periods, and the smells in the air were becoming very different. The air seemed to be getting cold faster with a heavier watery feel to it, which was making me colder. Since I was sure I could sense my way back when things got better, I headed off toward those lights. The sounds from the surrounding area were becoming louder and quicker, even a bit scary at times. So looking for shelter was my very first priority. Food and water were becoming a strong need as well.

Now while I was running and constantly searching the area, I noticed a few glaring eyes from ground creatures looking for shelter as well. *I hoped that I was not going to be their target for a fight or a meal!* That thought gave me shivers throughout.

Trying not to think too much about that and having a heightened awareness, I had to keep on track and run effortlessly along this dark road. If it were not for some of the light still coming from that big ball above, it would have been much harder to see my way. I do remember coming upon a small pond of water. It was a little muddy, but the smell seemed okay. So I did lap some up. Mind you, it was nothing like the fresh, clean water that I had been used to. But it was something to lap, and it made me feel a bit better. This gave me some hope and made it easier for me to continue my way to find shelter soon.

I could hear in the not too far distance some squeaky, clanky noises and decided to head that way. It was the only other sound that I had heard in quite some time other than the loud, long, sometimes scary noises that were coming from where I didn't know. But it was there! The flashes of light coming from above also gave me some guidance. As I got closer to the squeaky, clanky noises, I noticed some very weird things in a gathering of some kind.

The first thing that I came upon and investigated were these long tilted boards sticking up in the air while leaning on a longer bar going across. Just then, a very strong wind came upon me, and the two boards started to move on their own. I was quick enough to move out of the way as they almost hit me. They just kept moving up and down as the wind came in stronger and from different directions. *What were they for?* I wondered?

As I turned, there were other things swinging back and forth, faster and faster. Everywhere, I seemed to escape one thing—something else was doing something else! I jumped onto something that was still, and then it too started to move. Instead of going up and down or back and forth, it went around and around. I tried to keep my balance but started to feel sick, especially since I didn't eat and had been tired. Every time the wind picked up, these things all started to move. I, for sure, had to get off this one and fast! I lost my balance and almost fell if it wasn't for the hard thing that I was leaning against. As it finally slowed some, I was able to get off and a good thing too! A real long bright light came from above, then a short time later, a really big cracking sound came from above also. For sure, this place was dangerous! As I jumped and looked around, I saw all these things moving so fast and in all different directions. I didn't know or understand what this place was. Must get away from here and find shelter. But not here, so where to go? Too many things going up and down, back and forth, round and round!

CHAPTER 18

No Where to Go

While I was trying to sense where to go, all at once, the water came pouring down from above. I was now very, very wet that even shaking the water was too much for me to shake off. With the light that came from above again, I was able to see a large opening that I could maybe stay in for now. I ran as fast as I could for it and just in time too! There was a big tree that I hadn't seen before until the light came upon it and almost hit me as well. The light hit the tree with such meanness that a big piece fell to the ground, almost hitting my tail. Woof, that was close! Why would the light be so mean to hurt the tree like that? Then again, I was happy that it didn't break something on me! Yeah, that was for sure! Anyway, I headed toward that opening and went in to only find that it had two openings. One end where I went into, and the other end where I could get out. Not much protection but better than being out there with the water coming down so heavily and that hurtful light too!

I could feel some of the wind blowing in here, but not like it was out there. It also wasn't very much protection, but for now, it had to do. Trying to settle myself down and get comfortable wasn't easy because this was so hard and not flat like my bed back with Mommy June. I could only turn in only one position, laying with my face looking out one end and my tail the other end. As the wind was coming in, it brought a biting harsh cold on my already-cold wet body. Even as I tried to curl and snuggle, it was difficult to keep warm. So I told myself that this was better than nothing. I sure missed my warm, cozy bed back home.

While being here, I could hear the noises coming from within my place, which, of course, seemed to bring back a flash of past memories. These noises were familiar to me as I remembered the time when I was so very hungry in that safe place where the first humans found me. Remember? Those same noises were coming from within me. This time, I wasn't as scared like before. After all, I am bigger, stronger, and smarter now. Yet, I just don't know why I keep finding myself in situations where I am alone, hungry, thirsty, cold, and lonely. While resting in here, I realized how, once again it came to me how much my real mom was missed. Where is she? How is she? Does she remember me?

In spite of all that was going on around me exhaustion finally put me to sleep. After sometime and not sure how long I slept for, I began to wake up, feeling very wet and very uncomfortable. At this time, it was still dark. There was smelly water that was coming into my protected space. And was filling up around my legs as I lay there. So much for comfort! Getting up immediately, I stuck my head out, only to find that things were worse out there! So I had no choice but to wait it out here. Even with all this muddy water coming in things were better in here than out there. So trying to get comfortable was the best that could happen. After all, I had nowhere to go!

CHAPTER 19

What to Do

The night seemed to be so very long for me to stay in that small wet, windy, cold place. Deep within, I could not stop shaking. If it were not for the light that came and went so fast from above or the loud noises that followed shortly after, for sure, this was the longest, unhappiest, uncomfortable time of darkness I had ever been in up to then. Sometimes the sound was so very loud, and other times, it seemed to be far away. Still, it was far better than being out there with noisy, scary things moving back and forth, up and down, spinning around, and maybe even falling on me!

Still laying down watching all the things going on, I would think about Mommy June and Phillip. Would I ever get back to them? I wondered? Regardless of not being able to get comfortable and dry, sleep finally overcame me again.

During my sleep time, I had very bad, scary thoughts of things of shadows moving in and out, up and down, big giant trees with long, long limbs coming after me. Strong winds with things blowing around me—so strong it was as if it was lifting me off the ground. I was running no matter, but where to go? I could not know! So much stuff was coming at me in all different directions with some things hitting and knocking me down at times. It was so scary! As I slept, I could feel deep within me the pounding in my chest as my legs were moving so quickly. I was trying to run away to a safer place but couldn't find anywhere to go. This seemed to go on and on and on for such a long time. It seemed like forever before I was able to find a place of comfort and rest.

Waking up sometime later, the light was bright with things being a bit messy out there. There was much silence and stillness. Then I remembered all those things that happened to me and was just happy to have made it through the darkness while being able to stay in this place rather than out there. Those things that happened to me, I wondered if those were my thoughts during the darkness or did they really happen? I never did know the difference. It was all so real to me. Yet I am still where I was when I first came here. So it must not have been real. Or was it?

It was time for me to be heading on my way back to Mommy June and Phillip. I was still pretty wet, cold, and hungry. As I left my place of discomfort and hardness, I could feel the wonderful warmth from that bright thing way above. While I was walking and searching my area, it was good to feel my body warming up, and the shaking inside was going away.

As I was continuing on my journey, it was getting hotter. Which made me want water and food much more! While walking, not running, I encountered all kinds of houses and a few things that were unfamiliar to me. When I saw people, I would hide so they wouldn't get me and keep me from my mission of getting back to Mommy June and Philip. Sometimes I was able to find some food in a garbage can or some pieces on the ground. Water was a bit harder to come by.

This one time, I found myself in the back of a house, looking for water when a dog, who must have lived there, came charging after me. Before I realized what happened, we were in a fight. He didn't even give me a chance to allow him to sniff me or me him. So mean! He was a rather big guy and fast. I really didn't know that I could fight like that. Guess, when your life is in danger, you'd do anything to stay alive. Plus the play fighting with my brothers and sisters came in handy as my instincts kicked in. I sure did my very best in this mean, fast fight where we both got some good nips in. For some reason, we both stopped the fight, looked at each other then we both turned and went on our way. That was so weird and scary as well. I did feel a bit bruised but knew that I would be okay. Also, that taught me to be more aware of my surroundings. Remember to look up and all around!

This place was bigger as I was having trouble finding a way out of all these hidden paths. The houses looked alike in many ways—not much was different.

All I knew was that I had to find my way out of this place real soon.

Now one brightness, I found myself getting some food from another garbage can and found a thing that seemed to have some water in it. While I was trying to get some of the water, my instincts told me danger was nearby. When I looked up and around, there were two male humans slowly coming at me. This wasn't a good thing. Something in their eyes and movements wasn't right, and they carried a different scent. I ran away around the corner, only to find myself in a place that stopped. There was nowhere to escape. When I turned to head back, they were right there behind me. Oh, nowhere to run! So now I asked myself, "What to do?"

CHAPTER 20

No Way of Getting Back

As I was about to make a run for it, I noticed that one of the humans had a long pole with something that looked like a round leash. Just when I thought I could get through the two of them, that thing he was holding was quickly put around my neck and tightened. It tightened just enough to keep me from running away, but not hurting me. They were talking to me all the while this was going on. Since I had been around humans before, I didn't put up much of a fight but was now not going to be able to get back to Mommy June or Philip. Where they would be taking me, I didn't know. I felt kind of sad, anxious, and a little scared.

They were not rough with me, and that made this event a lot better. Both of them would just talk to me in a soft, kind voice. I followed them with the leash around my neck into a bigger and higher car, or a truck, I think it was called. It was higher off the ground and had a big door that opened. It wasn't hard for me to get into as they told me to jump up, and I did. They seemed surprised that I was so obedient. Then they guided me into a large crate with some blankets to lay on.

Aah, blankets to lay on. This was much better and more comfortable than I had been sleeping on for many darkness and brightness. It felt so good I could have almost relaxed and slept. Yet I needed to be aware of my surroundings.

There was another dog and a cat each in their own crate looking very sad and more scared than myself. As we rode, they both seemed to stay back farther in their crates, doing some shaking.

Except for the rather bumpy ride, it was very quiet. I felt good to be among humans who would now get me food, water, and shelter. Having to constantly look for food and getting into fights over food was not what I preferred. I also had to admit I did feel rather dirty, and for some reason, I was itching a lot. So a water wash would be good, as well as being petted and scratched. This itching was really starting to bother me a lot! There were these little tiny bugs that kept biting me, which was causing me to scratch myself in so many places. I tried biting them, but they were fast and just wouldn't leave me alone! It was getting harder and harder for me to be able to stop all this scratching, and my skin was getting rather sore now too. Maybe these new humans could help me with this. I sure hoped so!

We drove for a little bit and then came to a long stop. Everything was quiet until they opened the door again. What do you know? It was another dog! I tried to communicate with the others to let them know it wasn't as bad as they may be thinking. It would have been better for all of us if we were able to sniff each other. With not being of the same breeds, our communication was a bit off, yet we managed to understand each other somehow. This made us more relaxed and feeling pretty good until the new one came in all hyper and ready to fight one of us. For that matter, all of us, it seemed. The poor cat, this new dog was just ready to tear her apart. I was feeling so sorry for her, being so timid, lonely-looking, and now even more afraid. I tried to comfort her, but she wasn't having any part of it or of us. I decided that I would be ready to protect her when we got out of these crates. She reminded me of those little kittens I first got to know and love some time ago.

This new guy was pretty rough and tough. He didn't stop barking and was ripping up the stuff inside of his cage. *What was the matter with him?* I thought. I couldn't see much, but the sounds he made were not good for any of us. It surprised me how they were able to catch him or even get him into the crate.

Soon we were riding again, and when we came to another stop, the humans got out and started to open our crates for each us to get out. The rough dog stayed till the rest of us were out. We followed the humans into a place that was even louder with many other dogs. The rough dog was still barking lots. They left the cat in her crate and took her to a completely different area. In my sadness and concern for her, I was never able to protect her, nor did we ever see each other again. They took me directly to a room where two other humans were. Then put me up on a table and began to check my whole body, inside and out. They also sprayed me with something that felt kind of cool and comforting. After a few minutes of that stuff on me, to my relief, it seemed to ease my scratching a bit. I wasn't too fond of the sharp thing I felt go into my leg that pulled out some red stuff in a little bottle. Being in that little bottle and closed up, it was hard for me to smell what it was exactly that was taken out of me. I understood some of the words they were saying, like, "He seems pretty healthy in spite of some cuts and scratches, poor guy. These fleas are doing a number on him." That's what must be the name of those things that were causing me to itch. They called me a good boy and kept saying the name Blue to me. I was given the name Blue, because I had one blue eye and one brown eye. I was also a bit on the skinny side, they said, but that they were sure after cleaning me up, I would make a fine addition to a new home. But wait a minute, I was hoping that I could get back to Mommy June and Phillip who needed my protection. All they needed to do these humans was to clean me up, feed me, and let me go back on the road again. Now if they weren't going to do this for me, then wait just a minute, I would have no way of getting back!

CHAPTER 21

Including Me

After a while of being checked over, they took me to a big container that was filled with water and began to wash me. They scrubbed me all over, then rubbed and scratched by body. Wow! The water was so nice and warm too! Boy, did it feel really good! Unlike the water that came down from above when I was laying in it throughout the darkness that time. That was so cold and dirty. This was soooo good, and I loved the scrubbing, being talked to, and just feeling clean again. I thought this was going to go on for some time until I noticed the other dog that was with me in the big car was coming in to be washed. Guess, we all get this done. It was really good for us to have this washing. It is a pretty hard life having to fend for yourself all the time and wondering if you would be eating, where you might sleep—if you even could—trying to stay dry, and not get into a fighting match with another creature who wanted to take your food or possibly might want you to be their food! Yeah, you just stop and think about this for a moment! Scary, right?

Anyway, I reluctantly got out, was dried off, and then I felt warm air coming at me. They had something in their hand that was loud and warm. It was weird, but the warmth was, again, a good feeling. When all was done, they sprayed me again with some stuff and put another collar around me in addition to a new one. They said the old collar had to go, and this new one would be better. I understood them to say this should also help keep away those pesky fleas and any possible ticks. Not sure what a tick was, but I was just grateful for the attention and feeling better. So now I hoped to get something to eat and drink. This would be a perfect adventurous day for me to end with feeling clean, dry, a full belly, and a cozy place to sleep. I was getting really tired, and a nice warm bed would be so wonderful at this point. Aahhh, food and sleep!

We walked through a very noisy section with many other dogs barking trying to get my attention. One was saying welcome, another was saying, "Watch out, buddy," yet another was just so happy to have another one like me to have as a new friend, and others were wondering who I was and how I got there. So much going on at one time! Gosh, this was not what I needed now.

As we reached an empty cage, the human opened it and guided me inward. It was hard, long with a small blanket on the side, and on both sides were others that were so noisy with nonstop barking. Guess, this really was not what I expected, and now for sure, I wanted to get back to Mommy June and Philip.

It took some time for everyone to get fresh water, and a bowl of food was brought in as well.

The food wasn't what I was used to, but I was grateful it was here and didn't have to go hungry again. After we all ate, a few of us got to take turns going outside, do our business, and play. While outside, I had a chance to meet some of the others one on one. We got along very well, did some play, running and jumping on each other. Gotta say that it was fun.

This brought back memories of my real family when I was little. It had been so long since I got to really play around like that, and everyone seemed to be so friendly. When this was done, we were brought back to our very own places. In a short while when we were all done outside, the place became darker and rather cozy. By this time, almost everyone seemed to settle down and were ready to sleep, including me.

CHAPTER 22

Looking at Me

When I awoke due to the nonstop noises going on, I saw things were getting rather busy. Every time someone came into this area, so many would start barking and would just not be quiet. Boy, what a busy, noisy place! Was this going to be like this all the time? I wondered.

So one by one, we were allowed outside for a while. When I returned after doing my special thing, there was food and fresh water already waiting for me. That was nice. I couldn't believe how hungry I was and just couldn't seem to get enough. I did notice that there was a little more in there than what I had the time before. After I ate and rested, they opened my door for me to go outside again. Many were now with me, where we were able to stay out longer to do whatever we wanted. Since I didn't get a chance to sniff around and check out this place before, I decided to take this time now and do it. I also got to meet my new friends again. This place seemed to be quite safe. I felt more relaxed to run, play, chase the others, and do more fun things. Most of us played, chase a lot, and there were some toys to tug on with one another. One thing I noticed is that the brightness from above was so nice and warm on my body. The fresh air brought so many nice smells into my senses. It seemed like a perfect time to be here with no worries.

Having to go back into my private cage was not the happiest of times for me. It felt so confining. After being on the road so much, I needed to have more room to explore and be free.

Going into a confined cage was truly bothersome to me. This part I didn't like, which made me a bit sad, not by much, but still, just a bit. I seemed to know myself well enough to know that, in time, I would be able to settle in anywhere. Anyway, things seemed to always be changing for me. You just never know what's going to happen next.

Being in this place was something like the time I was with my first human family. Only here it was different. We were all pretty healthy, and there were a lot more of us living among each other.

I seemed to be popular with the humans who worked here. No one else like me, you know, my breed, seemed to be living here since the other one left. It didn't take long before they kept calling me Blue. A name that I began to answer to. They took me out for one-on-one walks while doing a lot of direct talking to me. Calling me by my new name, petting me, and even giving me hugs as we stopped to rest and look around. As we walked, they would be telling me stories about themselves or things around the area. It was nice being talked to and not just walked. One time, it brought back the memory of Jackie. I hoped she was doing good, and maybe someday, I would get to see her again. She had a special place in my heart, and I did miss her. When I think of her, I remember licking the water coming down from her eyes the last time we were together. It almost seems as if I can even taste them still. Gosh, I do miss her! Seems like when I remember, there are a few special humans whom I do care a lot about. It must be that love thing that Jackie told me about. When I think of her especially, my insides feel funny. Not a laughing kind, or a sick, or scary kind but just an enormous amount of joy and really good feelings—almost like these good feelings and emotions are too much to handle. Imagine that? Feelings and emotions that are too much to handle! It seems, at times, so overwhelming for me, especially in my chest area. It's like my insides feel beyond what I can explain. Maybe you know what I'm talking about?

Another thing, it was odd that most humans, whom my mom said to be careful of, were actually pretty good to me. I had a close relationship with most. Or maybe she was referring to a human like Daddy Joe. Yeah, that might have been it. I guess like us, dogs, who are not always nice, like that one who was in the big car before we got here and the one who attacked me that time, there are humans like that too. Hmmmm!

All right, I guess I got off the track a little bit. I'll get back to my memories now.

Another thing about this place that was different from any place I had been before was that there always seemed to be many humans coming in and out at special times of the brightness—again, like just before I went to live with Mommy June, Daddy Joe, and Philip.

Oh no, this must be what is going to happen to me again! I remember thinking. Like I said, you never know what's going to happen next and who's going to be looking at me.

CHAPTER 23

New Buddies

Once again, I found myself staying in another place for many, many brightness and darkness. However, during this time, there was this young boy who would come to see me a lot and take me out. This boy was bigger and older than Philip for sure and called Dean. We would have so much fun whenever we got together. He took such great care of me—so much that I could feel deep love and admiration from him toward me. There was something about him that was a bit like what Jackie and I had—but even deeper! Dean was funny, playful, caring, loving, and always talked to me. He gave me lots and lots of hugs, scratches, rubs on my belly, and lots of petting. I found that I wanted to be with him all the time.

One brightness, he brought to me a special person and said to me, "Now, Blue, I want you to meet a very special lady. I know you will like her. She is my mom! I think she is a great mom and someone who will love you as much as I love you!" He then said, "Mom, this is Blue, the one I have been telling you about." Oh, that was so nice, even when we are not together, Dean talks about me. How wonderful! I must be really special to him he brought his mom! Even with this wonderful event meeting his mom, to my surprise, a small pain I seemed to have felt inside of me and a sudden sadness. I realized then that I wished I could have had them meet my *mom*. She is a great mom too!

Now after these very profound thoughts, I realized that there was another something going on with me. This lady, whom he called

Mommy, also called *Serena*, had something very unique and special about her. This was very different from what I had ever experienced with any other human. She carried around her a special something, a different kind of energy, scent, and color about her. Dean was right. This lady I will like for sure! Her character seemed to be strong, somewhat firm, but at the same time, it was gentle and loving. Her colors around her body would change much as she spoke and as she allowed her feelings and emotions to express themselves. Wow! She carried a lot of brightness around her, and her chest area, I could see and sense a very, very warm love and lots of pinks and greens. Now you ask how do I know colors? That's because Dean would not only talk to me a lot as I said, but he would also teach me things. Colors and names of things that would be of great interest to me and sometimes not! Either way, I learned because knowing the names of colors came in pretty handy when I met his mom for the first time.

Besides noticing her energy and the colors that she carried, I felt very comfortable and relaxed around her immediately. I also felt a deep sense of something toward her. I knew, at this point, I would always protect her no matter what. She immediately came to me and knelt down so I could sniff her and check her out closer. Then she began to talk to me very lovingly and gave me a few good scratches behind my ears and down my neck. Wow, that was great! She sure did have great nails and found just the right spots where I loved to be scratched the most. We hung out for a while, and I was surprised that she took me for a walk while Dean stayed behind. She was a bit quiet every now and then while we walked. I think she was observing me, and I felt a bit self-conscious. Yes! A dog can feel self-conscious. You didn't know that, did you? See, even you learned something today! Ruff, ruff, meaning, haha!

Anyway, when she did talk, it was about different things we saw on the walk. Oh, one time, she took off on a run, and I loved it. We seemed so connected with the speed and the timing of it all, like I knew exactly what she wanted and when. She was so pleased with me that she began to laugh, and her face lit up, as well as her chest area even more than before. Wow, she was so pretty in all her colors, expressions, and laughter! Yep, I really do like this mom person.

We returned to my home, and soon Dean and his mom had to go. Boy, I felt so very sad and alone. It felt like I just lost my special family and new buddies.

CHAPTER 24

What a Surprise

When I next saw Dean, he seemed a little different. He was more joyful and playful than his usual self. There was definitely a special excitement about him and something mysterious. We got to spend our usual time together. He took me for a walk and brushed me with a nice brush that felt real good all over my body. Then I noticed he was carrying with him a collar and a leash that I hadn't seen before. It smelled different, only his scent along with other humans on them— no other dogs' scent.

Dean was so busy doing things that I was beginning to sense that he was forgetting about me.

But that's silly, I told myself. He loves me. Oops, where did that come from? Well, I do feel he loves me! He came over to me, knelt down in front of me, and looked me right in my eyes with a strange look on his face. He put his hands on either side of my head and so lovingly said to me, "Blue, I love you so much that I am going to take you home with me forever. You will never have to go to another home again."

What! What did he just say? Did I hear him right? He said it again. Oh my! I did hear it right! I got so excited that my tail would not stop wagging, like it had its own control. I started to jump up and down, and then I did a circle, Dean just knelt there watched me with a big smile on his face with lots of laugher coming from him. I couldn't help myself I just had to jump on him, all I could do was lick him and lick him. I was so happy! He fell to the floor, laughing and trying to hug me. I just couldn't stop being so excited. Really, a home, a home, a home to never worry about leaving again! I couldn't believe what I heard him say! But I know he said it! Ruff, ruff, ruff, ruff, ruff, and so on. Happy, happy, happy!

It was going to take a couple of days according to what Dean was telling me, but it didn't matter. This was something that I wanted, and waiting a couple of days was fine. It was exciting, and I got to say goodbye to my friends anyway. I felt a little saddened. Some of them had been there much longer than me and wanted to know if they could come with me. I was confused and could only tell them that this was not my decision to make. They seemed so put off by this, it was a very sad time. I tried my best to stay happy for them and tell them that if they couldn't come with me, someday soon, they would be with a family too! That seemed to help them be less sad.

The next day, I got to see Dean only for a brief time here and there. He was so busy doing this and that. He hardly had time for me. I was getting a bit concerned. He was acting like he forgot about me and that he was taking me home with him. Oh my, did he change his thinking? I must try to stay relaxed and in control. I sensed he might change his mind and think that I shouldn't go home with him. Oh, on a second thought, really, he wouldn't—he couldn't! He said he would, and I trust him. It is only my being nervous that I am sensing these silly things. I must be a good boy like he would say many times that I was. Yes, that is what I will do. Just be me, a good boy!

This day (or light like I used to call it, brightness, I now know it to be called a day) seemed to be one of those very long days, like the ones I experienced in the past—only worse! You see, I finally have a home, you know, a real home that someone wants me to be with them forever. This is different from all the places that I had been to so far. Forever! This is what was told to me from the very beginning by Dean. Forever! Do you have any idea what this means? Forever!

I will be with Dean, his mom, Serena, who is great, and I now know that he has a brother, Barrett, whom I haven't met yet. It is just going to be the three of them and me. No other human daddy who will hurt them or me, at least that is what I was to understand; he never mentioned a daddy. No one to hurt them. Like the daddy, you remember Joe, who would hurt Philip and his Mommy, June? Boy, I sure do hope they are okay. Now, mind you, all daddies are not mean. Daddy Joe was very nice until he would drink that water stuff from those bottles. After all, daddies are very important to have around.

Anyway, I waited and waited, but it seemed forever. I finally saw him coming to my cage. Yeah!

He was whistling while he was walking toward me and walking fast. I saw the leash in his hand. Oh, we were going for a walk finally. We were going to spend some time together this day. Now when he did reach me, he was talking so fast that I could hardly understand what he was saying, except for a few words here and there—home, Blue, mommy, now. Then he said it again as he was opening up my cage. It all became so clear. He said, "Blue, Mommy was able to get you to go home with us now."

"Yes, Blue, now!"

I couldn't believe what I was hearing.

He said home with them now! I was so happy. What a surprise!

Ben loving the deep snow
and the wonderful woods.

1995 Benjamin just
over 1 years old.

Ben and Pickles—just playing around.

Jake—just can't get enough of me.

Jake always liked being
behind the wheel.

2003—We're ready to come in!

Ben is inviting Jake to come and play.

CHAPTER 25

What a Place

Oh wow! Dean put that leash on my collar, then grabbed my bowl and bedding at the same time. I was so happy that I didn't pay much attention to all the others at first. They were barking at me to have a wonderful life, to remember them, some were asking still if they could come with me, and a few others just looked at me so sadly and quietly as I past them by. I could only look back at them as I was walking faster with Dean down the corridor toward the door while seeing all those beautiful faces and eyes looking at me, leaving them behind. I felt so sad yet so happy at the same time. Then through the door we both went.

Mom Serena was there waiting for us at the big desk. She had on this beautiful smile and glowed with such light around her. Sometimes I could see this light around Dean too! I wondered why they had this so much? It sure was a nice feeling to be around them. After a few minutes of them all talking, Mom, Serena bent down and talked directly to me, saying, "Well, Blue, you are now called Jake from this moment on. You will be coming home with us, and you will be a part of our family. You will have a wonderful life being with us and really never have to worry about going to another family. So, Jake, let's get started."

Soon off we went—Mom, Dean, and me—outdoors to the parking lot, and into their car, I went. Yep, I get to ride in a car. Yeah! It's been a while since I rode in a car. I got to ride in the open back with some kind of a gate between myself and my new family. It was nice that I wasn't put into a crate or tied up—just got to be free in this nice but small space with nothing blocking my views. There was wonderful fresh air coming in through the open window where Dean was sitting. This was real nice! I felt protected here, and all this felt so good and right. I am sure that as long as I behave myself, this is going to be my new home forever.

Now we didn't go too far before we stopped, and they took me out. As I sniffed and looked around, I could sense pleasant surroundings. There was a lot of grass and play area. Dean was so excited I could tell by the way he was talking to me. I could hardly pay attention because there was so much to take in. He took me for a walk around the place, and I noticed mom watching us. She looked so happy. There was a garden that Dean told me not to go into. I couldn't anyway—it was fenced off. I could smell other creatures had been here as well, especially other dogs. Some scents I wasn't familiar with and was very curious about. Although I was on the leash and curious enough to want to know, I was not going to be caught again in a bad situation as I did when I was just a pup and lost my first family. Oh, that memory! Things were too exciting for me now to go back into those memories. As we continued to walk around, I noticed there were lots of trees in the back, especially on the one side. There were lots of them that made it harder to see what was on the other side. He said that we could go for a walk in them someday. Oh wow, I never went into a place with all those big trees before— something to look forward too. But for now, there was so much for me to see and all the different smells right here. There were other houses that Dean told me about a little farther away from us, and we could still see them clearly because there weren't to many trees. After walking around and exploring with Dean while still on the leash, he started to head inside his house. He said this was his home, I mean, he actually said, "Our home." Now just stop for a minute! Did you just hear what I said? "Our home." He said "our home!" Boy, I could hardly stop my tail from wagging so much!

We went inside our home, and while he still kept the leash on me, he took me into the different rooms. I was too excited to care about the leash still being on me. I got to explore each and every room while Dean explained to me what to do and what not to do in it. Not sure I will remember, but he was a bit firm. He told me to not go into a certain room because it had to stay dog fur clean due to an allergy his brother has. I didn't understand what allergy meant, though. Dean spoke to me like I understood everything. That was interesting. Boy, this is a big home, and I get to be a part of it! I get to go to almost everywhere I want and whenever I want. This is true freedom!

I forgot to mention before that I did notice when I first arrived, there was a definite strong smell of other creatures who were in every room that I went into. Hmmm, why is this so strong? I wondered. One was one of the same scent I smelled outside while we were walking. So who were these other creatures and where were they? You know, it was similar to some of my friends' scents back at the place we just left.

He then brought me back downstairs took off the leash and had another little talk to me. Mom came over too and began to scratch my head and neck then said a few words to me as well. I understood most of them but more importantly was how gentle and loving they were both talking to me. They started to talk about another pet they said they have. His name is Benjamin, and he is like me, they said. What do they mean like me? Then they said I would have a new brother, but he was not there right now. He was at the vet and would be back soon, so I could have a chance to settle in before he came home. They said I was to be nice to him, and we must get along. This is his home too.

"Now, Jake, we also need you to know…"

Hmmm, what was going to happen now? Their energy seemed a bit different and more concerned now.

"Living with us in this home are other pets. One you know as Benjamin and the other is Pickles, he is our cat. So right now, he is hiding somewhere, and when you see him, please be a good boy to him."

I guess they didn't know that from my past, I know what cats are and their babies are called kittens. I know, I'm so smart! So they started to call out for this Pickles. Mom saw him, she went to pick him up and brought him over to me. She held him securely while we both got a chance to sniff each other. Okay, he didn't seem so bad, and he did remind me of the little ones that I used to take care of a while back. Pickles didn't seem to be too happy to have me there, so he decided to hiss at me. Silly him, I didn't understand what he was saying, but I figured out he was noting that he was here first and not to mess with him, and all will be fine. Well, that was a bit bossy. But we will see as times goes on. So I just let it be. Mom spoke to him gently till he calmed down. She held him for a while, and we got to know each other a bit more. I actually had no problem with him, and he finally understood that I was not going to hurt him. When she put him down, we stared at each other for a bit, sized each other up again now that we were able to move freely among each other. As we moved between each other, Pickles came over to me and started to rub himself against me. Wow, after his reaction toward me before, this was interesting, and it felt so nice of him to do this. I felt real comfortable to be with him as well. When I gave him a lick on his head, he looked up at me with such appreciation in his eyes.

Dean and Mom seemed to be really pleased while sitting together with a big smile, saying, "Awe!"

They were so cute themselves I couldn't resist giving them each a quick lick!

Soon Dean took me into the kitchen where he showed me a bowl of food and water for me to eat. I was too excited to be able to eat anything right now. I also noticed another bowl and water on the other side of the kitchen and went over to that as well. Dean said this bowl belongs to Benjamin, and the one I was just at, which he took me back to again, was mine. Oh well, guess I was hungrier more than I thought. He gave me a nice bowl of food to eat and fresh water to drink. I sure did eat it all up. Yummy!

I was still so excited, but with all this new stuff going on, I have to admit I was getting tired. They also had a nice bed for me in a cozy corner so I can see everything. In fact, there seemed to be two of them close together. Guess this Benjamin and I get to share this home and many things. I have to admit that this home was nice, it had a nice smell to it, and was very comfortable. I decided to go to bed for now and rest. Before closing my eyes, I reflected on all that happened today. Boy, what a place!

CHAPTER 26

Will I Stay or Will I Go?

I had a great night's sleep. Feeling so rested and relaxed, I finally got up and indicated to them that I had to go out. But where do I do? Which place will take me outside to do my business? "*I must not mess in this house,*" I told myself.

Mom came around the corner and stated, "Oh, you're up. Hope you slept well, Jake. Come this way to go outside. Come on, Jake. This way."

Mom put on my leash, and out we went. Wow, what a nice day. No noises from above, the day was bright, and the air was fresh and smelled great! We walked around a bit. I marked different places. Mom kept saying something about a special collar she was going to get for me so I can come in and out of the house by myself and she wouldn't have to worry about me running off the property into the street or woods. Hmmm, wonder what it was all about. A special collar? But it would be nice to be able to come and go as I pleased. This place is getting better and better! Wow!

As the days went on, I got to go in and out with either Mom or Dean. I had tasty meals and great walks. I also took a stroll around the house by myself and found Pickles a few times sleeping. Boy, he sleeps a lot! I wanted to play, but he just wanted to sleep. Mom gave me a bone to chew on, and this helped me from being bored. You know, this is really a nice home to be in, but I began to feel a little bored. In the other place, I did have the others to talk to and play with outside. But this place is very quiet and peaceful to be in.

Dean did stop by and said he had to go but would be back later. He was sorry that I couldn't go with him, he said. It came to be that he was gone most of the day, and mom was a bit busy on that phone thing. She talked a lot to someone, but I never got to see who she was talking to. Very interesting that phone thing. Very! Mom would call me over every now and then and pet my head or scratch my head and back. It felt real good too!

Then later in the day, Mom called me over and said she had to go out, and I was to stay home for now. She was going to get Benjamin. Oh boy, Benjamin! I heard lots about him. Great, someone to play with now. I just love to play and play. Know what I mean? Do you?

After she left, I went to find Pickles. He was high up on a bed near the very top of the wall. He jumped down, and we got to chase each other for a bit. As I ran around the corner to chase him, which was lots of fun, my tail hit something, then I heard a bang and weird noises. I stopped, turned, and oh no! What just happened! I have no idea what it was, but it was on the floor in many pieces. Did I do this? What was this? Am I going to get into trouble? Pickles came by and said that I broke it.

"But broke what?" I said.

He said, "It didn't matter. It was broken, and I was going to get into trouble."

"Oh no, what did I do? I didn't mean to!"

This was not good for me, especially since this was my first time being left alone. Pickles didn't help much by saying over and over, "You're going to be in trouble when Mom gets home. You're going to be in trouble when Mom gets home. You're going to be in trouble when Mom gets home."

He was walking around me with his tail straight up in the air, like he was such a big shot! Not funny in any way!

Boy, I didn't mean to do that. What was going to happen now? Were they going to bring me back? Were they going to just toss me out? Or take me for a car ride and tie me to a tree like Daddy Joe did? Oh no! What am I going to do? Not sure, being a bit scared and sad,

I just laid down on my bed and waited until it was time for mom to get home. It seemed to take forever.

I heard a rumbling noise and could sense that Mom was home with Benjamin. Now I just knew it was time for me to be leaving this home, which I thought was going to be mine forever. Now it's no more for me! I was a bad boy, and now I am going to have to leave. I am soooo sad. Do I just stay? Do I get up and go greet them with joy like I would have done anyway? What should I do? The real big question is, Will I stay or go?

CHAPTER 27

Just Real Cute

Well, I decided to be brave and go greet them as I would have otherwise. I'm truly happy to see Mom and wanted to meet Benjamin. So there I was, standing on the other side of the door, very happy with my tail wagging. Hearing them on the other side, I could already pick up on Benjamin's scent. When the door opened, yeah, there they were, Mommy and my new playmate, Benjamin. He seemed a little taken back by my presence, but nonetheless, there he was with some weird thing around his head. He seemed to be a little happy, but I could sense he wasn't feeling well. Mom immediately said things, like, "Easy, boys, and be nice to each other." She directed us toward the open part of the room, where we began to check each other out more closely. I've seen that kind of a thing that Benjamin had on his head from the places I've been before on other creatures like me. Glad I'm not wearing one. It is so hard to get around with one of those on your neck and head. Makes it very difficult to sniff, eat, drink, scratch, and play. Every time he came close to me or tried to sniff my backside as I was doing him, that thing would just slam into me. It kinda hurt too. He was having a tough time walking around with it, unable to see much while banging into different things and walls as he tried to get around. Poor guy! If not feeling well wasn't bad enough, that thing made it worse. He seemed to be miserable and a bit wobbly.

Other than this particular issue, Benjamin seemed to be a gentle kind of a dog who didn't show any fear of me at all or wanted to attack me. That was a great thing too. Yet he didn't seem to be too interested in wanting to get to know me right now. After sniffing each other for a bit, he went straight to his bed and quickly off to sleep. Well, at least we got to meet each other, and when he is feeling better, I guess we can play together.

Even while Benjamin was sleeping, I was able to get in a few more sniffs before I heard a loud, "Oh no! What happened here? Who did this?"

So much for my distraction! Time to face the music, as I've heard this expression a few times. So instead of going over to the place of the broken thing and Mom, I just went to my own bed and waited for the punishment. What could I do, really? There was no way of me telling her it was an accident, that my tail hit it when I was playing with Pickles. Really! What could I do? How could I even tell her? She doesn't understand my language. I knew that she was going to be really mad at me and punish me for sure. She came over and looked at me real stern with her hands on her hips. I couldn't really look at her for too long, so I turned my head away because I felt so bad and put my paws over my eyes so I could pretend she wasn't there and this wasn't happening. Then I heard her making noises, but I was kind of afraid to look. Was this going to be my reason for them not wanting me anymore? When I did finally peek at her, she had her hands over her mouth while making a weird noise. Was she crying? I saw no water coming from her eyes. So what was happening just then? Her eyes were wide, her body was shaking some, and she seemed to be really happy. I believe she was laughing, yeah, that's it—she's laughing! Laughing, which means she's not mad at me. But why? I wondered. Why isn't she mad at me? It's good, but why?

When she finally took her hands away from her mouth and took a deep breath, with a gleam in her eyes, she said, "Jake you're so funny, and I see you know how to work it! You think you're so cute by putting your paws over your eyes? Well, I have to say you sure did a number on me! How can I be mad at you now?"

Oh, so this is what I did! Cute, she thinks, hmmm gotta remember this one.

Guess, it pays to be innocent. She gave me a few pats on my head, said a few other things, and left me to rest. Wow, this was close, and I'm off the hook for this one. I must be pretty lucky or just real cute!

CHAPTER 28

Territory

So during the darkness, things became pretty interesting. Benjamin wasn't doing too well, and Pickles was running all over, then hiding, then running again. What was going on? Apparently, Pickles just didn't like seeing Benjamin so sick with throwing up and some weird pooping he was doing. It did smell a bit different and thought I shouldn't go near it. Otherwise, I thought it to be fine. All the noise going on caused mom and Dean to come running over and check things out. When I looked at him, he was worse than when we first saw each other. Mom and Dean became very busy trying to keep everyone calm and cleaning up after poor Benjamin. I didn't understand or know what exactly was wrong with him. Then I heard mom talking to someone other than us, but I couldn't see who it was. She was holding a small item in her hand to her ear, which, of course, I know was her phone. Interesting how she talks so much, yet I don't ever see anyone else there. Maybe she's really talking to me, and I'm supposed to answer her? So when I got close to her to be sure of this, she was still talking, this reminded me of the time, when I thought another dog or maybe one of my brothers would disappear in the mirror back at the other place. I could see but couldn't touch, which, of course, it was me all the time. Remember, that's when I got to see how nice-looking I am. Remember that? Anyway, like now, I can hear her talking but have no idea who she's talking to. Things sure are strange.

Let's get back to poor Benjamin. Soon Barrett came home from being away at school. As he looked around, he was surprised to see me. This was the first time we got to meet each other.

He said, "Oh, we have a new dog! What's his name? Is he friendly? When did he get here?" Then as he looked further, he saw poor Benjamin. "Oh, what is going on here, Dean? Who's mom talking too?"

Dean tried to answer as many questions while trying to clean up and assist Benjamin. I was told to stay on my bed and be a good boy. Barrett came over to me quickly and allowed me to get a good sniff of his scent along with a good pat on my head and a quick scratch on my neck before he asked what he could do to help. That was a nice scratch, and I got a good sniff of him. Yep, he's going to be just fine to be with as well.

Things were busy, and when mom finished with her phone, she gathered Benjamin up and left our home. Dean and Barrett continued to clean up. When all was done, both of them came over to sit with me. I got lots of scratches, rubs, hugs, petting, and great attention! Dean was telling Barrett all about me and that they also wanted to surprise him. Barrett seemed really happy to have me, even Pickles finally joined us. Wow! This was so nice and so great to have this attention and family time.

It seemed like a very long time before mom came home. She then told us that Benjamin was going to be fine. He apparently had a delayed reaction to a new medication. They stabilized him, and he is going to be spending the night at the vets. He is going through much—first, with his surgery removing those lumps, his ears with the hematomas from shaking his head so much, and now this reaction.

"Well, Mr. Jake," mom said, "guess you came to us at a very busy time. Don't worry. Benjamin will be back to himself real soon, and you can have a playmate. In the meantime, you have Pickles and us!"

That night, we all seemed to sleep pretty well, knowing that Benjamin was going to be all right. Even though they felt he was going to be okay, he was going to spend another night at the vets just to be on the safe side, I heard mom say. In the meantime, I was taken outside for many walks and got to know my surroundings better. It was nice to be outside like this. Dean and/or Barrett would take me out and play that ball thing with me. The one where they would throw it, and I would get it to bring back to them, only to have them do it again and again. We had lots of fun, especially when mom came out to throw the ball.

One thing I noticed since I got here was that Pickles didn't come outside at all. I wondered why? I also noticed that they seemed to walk me in certain places. I get to walk around to the edge of the property, that's what Dean would call it, and was told not to go off it. It would be the same areas of walking around when I would first go out and again just before I went inside. My scent was getting stronger within these areas, and my markings were a definite warning to others that I am now here. Too good to be true, you might say, but it sure is! I am able to offset any of Benjamin's scents too. What can I say, this is the nature of the territory!

CHAPTER 29

At Least So Far

1999 Benjamin and Jake becoming inseparable.

Well, the time came finally for Benjamin to come home. Even though he was still wearing that head thing, he seemed to be a lot happier and healthier. We even got to play a little bit and kind of did a little play chasing inside, but not much! I didn't want to knock anything over again with my tail. Please let's not go there now. Thanks.

Life seemed to be good living here with Dean, Barrett, and Mom. After many, many days and nights of being here, this one time when we were left alone, as we were many times, I noticed that there was this creature crawling on the floor but much smaller than me.

So naturally, I thought that I should get it before it did any damage. In the hallway by the little bathroom, as they call it, I noticed it went under a piece of flooring that was kind of loose. So guess what? Yeah, I went after it! Then scratched on that loose piece of flooring. I bit at it until finally, I got the bug creature. So, I did the most natural thing. I ate him up. He was tasty too! When all was finished, I noticed that a good piece of the flooring was missing and lots of pieces were all over. Would this be an oops moment? I guess I did a lot more than just getting rid of him, which I hope was okay? I did get the bug, they should be proud of me, and I did a pretty good job of helping them out. As I was making myself feel better, guess who came by and destroyed that moment? Yep!

Pickles came by, and again, he said, "You're gonna get into trouble! You're gonna get into trouble!"

Why does he have to repeat himself over and over! He is the most annoying. But then again, oh no! Did I do something wrong? Again? I was just trying to help! Oh, maybe he is wrong this time. I'm a good boy, and I do my best to help out around here. Really, I do! So we will just have to see about what Pickles said. In the meantime, I am going to play with my toys. I have lots of them. Bones, chew toys, stuffed animals to play with, balls, and tug toys that Benjamin and I play with a lot. That's my favorite toy because we really get to see who is the strongest and who can hold on the longest. I love playing with him! Pickles, he doesn't play like this with us. He just sleeps mostly, and sometimes the three of us get to play chase. But you know, it is nice when he sleeps next to me. It feels cozy and comforting for the both of us. Once in a while, all three of us will cuddle up together. This seems to be very special to my human family. They come over and say all kinds of sweet-loving things while taking pictures of us. We seem to have many pictures taken. We must be special. So back to playing with my toys.

It was late when mom came home. At first, nothing was said to me about the floor, so everything must be fine, and Pickles was mistaken. Then it came! Oh boy! Did it come! I heard my name spoken very loudly.

"Jake! Jake, what have you done now and why in high heavens did you do this to my floor? I know it was you! Jake?"

She came to get me and brought me over to the floor pieces. Even though she was mad, she took me by my collar and gently directed me to the spot. I am pleased that she was gentle even though she was mad at me, not like Daddy Joe when he grabbed me. Ohhh, that was rough on me and hurtful! Anyway, I looked at mom with solemn eyes and couldn't understand why she was mad at me. After all, I was a good boy and got that big bug for her. But how will she know what I did when I ate it? I have nothing to show her that I was doing it as a good boy!

She looked at me with a stern face and said, "Oh, Jake, you didn't know this, but this floor was going to have to be replaced anyway. Now I have no choice but to do it sooner." She paused then huffed and continued to say, "I guess this is pushing me to do it. Boy, you are sure lucky again, Jake! Really, though, I just don't have this time now. Yet what choice will I have. This is a mess!"

So I guess I was a good boy after all, and in a great way, I helped mom get started! Pickles wasn't sure what to say to me now!

Within a few days, mom was ripping up the old floor and getting it ready to put down another. She was working on it herself. She even put a new thing that they seem to sit on a lot in that little room. It think she called it a toilet. It took her many days to get it done because she only had time to do it when she came home from work. I guess she has lots of talent, as I heard Dean and Barrett talking about the work she was doing on the floor and that toilet thing. Thank goodness, everything worked out for the best. When mom finished, it all looked great and brand new.

In the meantime, I tried to stay aware of what I should and should not do. It seems a bit hard at times because I think I am doing something good or just having fun, and oops, there goes another one! You know, when I was on the road by myself, at least I knew I was my own boss and could do just about anything or go just about anywhere without getting into trouble. But I admit that it was lonely. Most of the time, I was dirty and hungry, scared at times, and not real comfortable finding cozy places to sleep and staying warm. So being in this home definitely has a huge plus, especially that when I do manage to do something wrong, at least I believe I am still loved, and they are not mean to me—at least, so far!

CHAPTER 30

Made No Sense to Me

The many days and nights that followed, Dean was still my buddy. We didn't get to see much of each other since he goes off to this school and work thing. I wondered what it was all about. He would almost every day come over to me after we spent time together then say, "Okay, Jake, I have to get off to school. Then after work tonight, we can spend time together again."

So that's how it went most of the time. Mom would just come over after feeding us, give us scratches, and hugs then leave for this work thing too. So why does she go to this workplace only while Dean goes to school and to work? Barrett said he is on some sort of vacation. So what is the difference? He takes me for my many walks outside in our yard and to other places as well.

One day, while Barrett and I were in our yard walking side by side with my leash attached, I suddenly stopped and noticed there was this great big dog, or so I thought. It was just standing there, staring at both of us and stood so very, very still. I wasn't sure at first if it was alive or not. It was much, much bigger than me and had these funny things coming out of the top of its head. Plus his smell was so different from any other dog I had met so far. I can remember now that I heard Barrett say, "Oh no!" I guess, he saw it too. But I was the one who first got so excited, and before I knew it, I went charging after it to see if it wanted to play and to find out what exactly it was! I think I broke the leash because I heard Barrett calling after me to stop, and his voice wasn't so much in my hearing range anymore. It was like I was a different dog. I just had this thing inside of me to go chasing after it. I couldn't stop myself for some reason. So I went into those woods and followed it for a bit. It was beautiful to watch as it did all the jumping, as if it was floating in the air, over all those high bushes and fallen tree so easily. *Wow!* I thought. I wanted to do that too!

When I finally couldn't find the creature anymore, I stopped. Boy, that thing was real fast! Yeah, even faster than me. I couldn't believe how fast! I thought I was a fast runner, but that thing took off like nothing I have ever seen before.

As I stopped, I realized I had no idea as to where I was. So, I just waited and rested for a few moments just thinking about that amazing creature and its pure beauty! I also realized that I had a really good run and was breathing heavily. Then, in the distance, I heard Barrett calling after me. Good, I wouldn't get myself into trouble by getting lost like the first time when I was just a young pup. I followed my scent back as well and kept on hearing Barrett's voice getting closer and closer. When he saw me, his face lit up, and I ran right into his outstretched arms. Boy, he was so happy to see me. That was a nice surprise and made me feel real good. Then he did seem to scold me a bit but was still so happy at the same time. He told me that I was not being good by going after that deer. Deer? What is a deer? Oh, that creature I was chasing was a deer. Good to know. That was so much fun chasing him. I just wanted to catch him and play. Maybe next time, he will chase me! Then Barrett put the leash on me as best he could since I broke the connecting part, he said. Now they will have to buy a new one.

He said to me, "Oh, Jake, you are a handful at times! Still, I love you. You know, Jake, people say to get rid of you…"

What? People say to get rid of me? Oh no! What do they mean get rid of me anyway?

Did it mean I would be going for another car ride, tied to a tree and left all by myself again? Are they going to really get rid of me? Now I am a bit scared. What will Mom and Dean say when they find out I was running after this so-called deer creature? Even though Barrett was still talking, I never did hear the rest of what he was saying to me. My thoughts were on his words of what people would say, and this was all I could think about on my way home. I tried to stay real close to Barrett and show him how much I loved him too! Yet those words stayed with me for some time as we walked back home.

Later that night, I heard all of them talking about my running after the deer and getting some kind of a fence. They were saying that it would keep me in the yard, and I would be able to go outside by myself after a while of training. They talked about wall fences, wire fences, and an invisible fence. I really had no idea what all those fences were about, but it was making me feel a little uncomfortable. The conversation was all about me. They were talking about expenses, time, training, and freedom. Now that word "freedom" I understood! The other words made no sense to me.

CHAPTER 31

What Do You Think?

A loving work day
with my boys!

Jake and Ben resting
from our walk—2003

Well, for some time now, nothing more was noted about the fence thing, and I think they may have forgotten about it too. Life moved forward, and we were doing lots more.

Mom said one day that she was going to take both Benjamin and me to work. Plus we had to go in the car to get there. Wow, a car ride and seeing what this work thing was all about too! What an exciting day we were going to have. Well, it turns out that mom worked for some kind of a doctor. Not the kind that took care of guys like me or other creatures. She was some kind of office manager, and as we drove, she explained to us what she did there. That was one of those special things about mom that I liked. She always talked to us. On this one particular day, she said the office was closed to patients while she did the billing and appointment recalls. Actually, this family always seemed to explain to us what was going on, which is what made us feel like one of the family for sure! Yeah, that was a great feeling and kept us close together. Being there that day was so nice. Mom would also take us for walks around the place. So we got to see new things. Okay, mom did take Benjamin to work before on many occasions, but this being my first time, well, it was exciting for me.

Overtime, we would go to work with her every now and then. Now this one particular time, Benjamin was still inside the office, and mom just took me for the walk. I needed to go marking fast. Anyway, on our way back on the sidewalk by the building, there was this mom and a little female human walking toward us. Mom stopped and talked to them. As I was facing the little female human, who happened to be about as tall as me, I quickly took a snap at her but didn't bite her or harm her in any way! No, not in any way! I just gave her a good warning. Mom was so surprised and quickly pulled me back.

"Jake, No! Bad boy, Jake," she said.

She said something to the lady and the little female, then off we quickly went back into the office. Mom then pulled me close to her, bent down, and questioned me as to why I would do such a thing and to a little child no less. She told me to never do such a thing like that again!

"But, Mom," I tried to say, "this little child might have been little, but I could sense that she was not a nice child. I knew she looked sweet, but inside, she was not a nice human. I was just warning her with my action to not hurt you."

Mom just didn't understand this. She was so upset with me that I might have bitten the little human, plus being confused and tried to figure out why I did that. After this event, mom seemed to be more cautious of me being around others. It kind of messed up my true freedom of walking on a leash without having to turn away from others coming near me. If only she understood that I was just protecting her. If only? (As time moved on, mom got to understand me more but still a slight bit cautious of me with others.)

Life was still very good, and the love I got was great! Dean, Barrett, and Mom always spent much time with us and as often as they could. We never felt lonely when they were not home either. We always had each other to play with, hang out with, we slept together, and just having lots of fun. Speaking of having lots of fun, I remember this one time. Gotta admit that Benjamin did get the short end of the deal, and maybe it wasn't really fun, at least not for him. Anyway, mom decided to leave us this one bone when they went out. What was she thinking? Oops, I guess she wasn't!

Well, we were all doing really fine while they were gone until Benjamin decided that he didn't want to share the bone. This caused us to have a little scuff before I finally got the bone. Pickles then did his usual lying on his bed, which, most of the time, he does anyway. Now when they got home, they came in from the downstairs entry and walked into the hallway. At first, all looked pretty good until mom went to say hi to Benjamin and noticed some blood coming off his ear and leg. Okay, I did get a bit rough, but he wouldn't give me my time with the bone! Besides, it really wasn't much blood. I only nipped him to show him that I am the boss, and he should share things. Besides, that's my version, and I am sticking with it for sure.

Actually, as I look back on this, I do feel a bit bad as to how I treated him over the bone. I'll have to find him and tell him that I'm sorry for hurting him. He was always good to me and was actually like a pup brother to me. But the interesting part was when mom walked into the hallway and noticed blood spots on the floor, walls, closet door, and going up the stairway walls. It looked a lot worse than what really took place. It got that way because Benjamin shook his head after I nipped his ear and leg. So it splattered all over! Again, I was taken aside, and for sure, they figured what had happened and gave me another talking to.

As I look back on those times, I sure did get a lot of talking to. What was going on with me that I needed to be talked to so much? (Maybe I'll figure it out in time as I continue with my life's story. On the other hand, maybe that is why I was called to this particular place and time in order to figure out this issue going on with me during those days. What do you think?)

CHAPTER 32

Swim or Sink

Ben being safe wearing his life vest while having fun.

1999 Jake 3 and Ben 5 yrs.old—loving our swims.

I always found myself watching mom a lot. She was always busy doing one thing or another yet still always found the time to spend with us. We would go out for walks and hiking in the woods—I really liked doing that. Mom would let us run for a bit then play this hide-and-seek game with us. That was so much fun! We would run ahead of her, then stop, turn around, and she would be gone! So we would then run back to where she was last, and all of a sudden, she would jump out from a hiding place and say, "Got ya!" This would give us a fun scare, and then Ben and me would jump all over each other. The walking would start again, and maybe another game of this would take place. I never knew when it would happen, though, so we were always on a fun guard and also always having to keep mom within our sight. Mom had this special whistle sound she made to alert us if we went too far from her. She was wise like that. Benjamin, in the beginning, would always be the first to turn around and start the search for her. I began to understand the importance of this game and finding mom as time went on. In addition to these walks and hikes, we went for many car rides, visiting playgrounds to play with other dogs, and going to special swimming holes or the beach. When we went to the watering places to get cooled off or just have lots of fun, Benjamin and I noticed how our fur coats and skin always seemed to get nice and clean on their own! I think mom knew this also. Besides, a good wash never hurt anyone.

Oh my! I just remembered this one time when I was just first learning how to swim. Now you actually thought that all dogs knew how to swim, didn't you?

So anyway, this one time, we went up to the lake where we could also go for a great walk and then swim or vice versa. Mom always kept us close to the shoreline with a very long leash. Benjamin seemed to know how to swim. He said mom taught him. I thought I did pretty good until this one time, mom decided to swim across to the little island not far from where we were starting out. She mentioned out loud that she had some very important items she was holding in one hand while swimming with the other, trying not to get them wet. Benjamin was doing really fine and kind of showing off. I started out doing well, but then for some reason, I started to sink. Mom told others later that she saw my back legs and back body start to sink further under the water, saw my upper body going down, then my neck and my face began to go under the water. She immediately said the heck with her things and put her free hand under my belly to support me. My legs and back were not in the right position to help me stay afloat. I was more important than the things she was holding up. (Awh, that was such a wonderful thing to hear her say.) So she held my back end up and swam with her other arm at the same time. We got to the island, which wasn't too far away to begin with. She held onto me and gave me a great big hug while talking to me. She was surprised that I didn't know how to swim and that she is learning much about dogs as well, thinking I would know automatically and realizing that she had another dog she needed to teach from the same breed. Not for anything she said, but all my past pets did know how to swim. However, this was okay, and she would love to teach me how to do this. In the meantime, we needed to get back to the other side, but in a few minutes, we would play a little then head back after a good rest.

Well, the way back was a bit harder for me. I felt a bit uncertain, and mom again had to hold up my bottom and swim with one hand. I started to sink faster. She did a great job. Before we got out on the other side, she turned to me, and while she was in a sitting position, I jumped onto her and placed each one of my front legs and paws around either side of her neck. I was more unsettled this time and just rested my head on one of her shoulders. I was hugging her in a sense. That was an experience I didn't want to go through again. Mom held me close, securely, and with such love for a few minutes. People were watching us, and she didn't seem to mind. My love for her was growing so much. Benjamin was showing off again while this was happening by swimming all around us. He seemed to be very happy, peaceful and, at the same time, really enjoying himself. It was nice to see how he was doing it. He wasn't afraid of this water as he was with most other things. Benjamin was so confident and made it seem so easy. I knew that if he could do it, then so can I!

From this experience, mom decided that she was going to get us doggie life vests. After they were bought, she took time to teach me how to be a stronger swimmer in my hindquarters, which, of course, helped me stay afloat. Wearing the life vest did make it a lot easier, and I had lots more fun. It was so scary for me to have to go into the deeper waters, but between the vest and mom's encouragement, it was much easier.

In time, mom would bring along this big flat float thing. It was kind of funny because Benjamin and I would climb on it while mom would push us around. We were floating on top of the water, getting a ride while feeling refreshed and comfortable all at the same time! Poor mom, she did all the work and would make funny comments about it too!

For example, "Is something wrong with this picture?" "How is it that you get to relax, and I get to do all the work?" "You guys have me wrapped around your paws when it comes to this." "You two deserve a break, and I do enjoy watching you having fun." She would laugh about these things too. Actually, we all had great times. That's when I finally learned to either swim or sink!

CHAPTER 33

Nice Human

There was this one special time when I noticed that mom came home from her day at work and did something different. You see, she usually came home, fed us, and if Dean and Barrett were home, we would all eat together, always following with some cleaning up and a walk. Then after some playtime, she would sit down, rub us and/ or give us scratches all over. Gosh, that did feel great! Mom would do some other things and afterward go to bed much later at night. However, this time, she fed us, took us for our walk, and since Dean and Barrett weren't here, we played only a short time while she talked to us about going out to do something with someone. Our scratching session was shorter too. Instead of doing all the usual things that follow, she went upstairs and lay in lots of water in that room she goes into to get wet. If I recall, I think it is a bathtub. Pretty sure, that's what it's called. Anyway, she was also happier than normal (not that she isn't usually, but this was different) and a bit more serious or nervous maybe at the same time. It was interesting to see her this way. Very unusual, I always sensed her to be strong and controlled. But this time, I could sense changes in her. At the same time, I would get these flashes of picture thoughts from her, but they weren't quite clear enough to understand at that particular time. (Picture thoughts is how we understand humans with special words as well.)

I was resting comfortably on the big bed with Pickles while Benjamin was on the floor, sound asleep. We all liked to stay together when mom was home. While I was getting all these strong flashes of her thoughts as she moved around doing all kinds of things, I finally understood what was happening. There was going to be a male human coming for her. With this new realization, I immediately jumped off the bed and ran downstairs, barking all sorts of things like, "Where are you?" "This is my mom. Where are you male human?" "You better not harm her, male human." "I am here to protect her." "Watch out! Be good to her!"

You see, I was uncertain of big male humans after being with Daddy Joe. Remember him?

With all my barking, mom came rushing down to calm me down. Actually, at this particular time, there was no one there at all! I had become too excited and reacted to what I was sensing from mom. It surprised her, my acting crazy. Once all was calm, we went back upstairs, and I continued to watch her. She was still happier and a bit nervous at the same time. I wondered why? If she was nervous, then there should be a reason for me to be protective. Right? Yet she told me to be nice, and that all is fine and okay. So why was she nervous and why was I to be nice? I kept my guard up just in case. Something was a bit strange to me, and I just didn't understand it. Yet, for sure, I just had to trust mom.

A little later, I heard a different noise that I wasn't familiar with coming onto our property. I always know the difference as to who is coming down the driveway by the different sounds of the things that they rode in. So this time, I waited a bit so I would not get mom upset although it was different when I heard the bell ring. Now for sure, it was time for me to take action! I just don't know what was getting into me with this particular situation. Why was I so ready to jump and run to the rescue for mom right now? It must be those Daddy Joe memories and the emotions that I still experience. It just had to be!

I've been there when many other humans came to the door, and I didn't become as protective as I was then. Okay, I did do some harsh barking, but not like this. Now there were two doors. One on the outside that when closed, you couldn't see through, and the other was some kind of a screen door, as they called it, that you could see outside and still let in light and wind and sometimes water when that came down from above. Rain, that's what it is called, I remember now. It's called rain. Anyway, when I saw this big male human, I just got so much more protective. When I got to the screen door, I jumped up as high as I could stand and faced him from my side, barking and sounding quite scary too! He immediately put his one hand on his side to try to keep me from pushing it open. His other hand was behind his back, trying to hide something from me. What did he have back there? There was a very nice smell to whatever it was he was hiding from me. But I couldn't get distracted from that smell at this time. While I was still standing on my hind legs, pushing on the screen door, I sensed that he seemed a bit scared. Good, then he knows I mean business! Yet I sensed almost immediately that he seemed different from Daddy Joe. As I continued protecting, I sensed that this human had a gentle energy about him. Mom came rushing down, took me aside, and calmed me. She noticed I was a bit more aggressive and decided to use this thing called a muzzle that would be placed around my mouth and head. Ever since the situation with the little girl and my reactions to other humans coming to the door, mom decided to be a bit more cautious.

She allowed this human to enter, and with the muzzle still on, I got a real good sniff. He waited for me to finish, which was smart of him, and then he placed his back hand down for me to sniff, then placed it upon my head, patted me, scratched my head, and behind my ears while talking to me. Wow, this was very smart of him, and he seemed to be calm and relaxed. While being closer, no screen between us and me being calmer, I sensed a pleasant energy that he carried within and around him. I let him continue with the petting and scratching because I'm no fool. The scratching felt so great, and I loved it!

By this time, Benjamin and Pickles came in, and Mom introduced all of us. This male human was known as Steve. By now, he took what he was hiding behind his back and gave it to Mom. She smelled them, had a nice smile on her face, said thank you to him, and we followed the two of them into the kitchen area. It was interesting because during the time we spent upstairs when she was getting dressed, one of her thoughts that I picked up on was what

Steve brought to Mom. She knew this beforehand. Wow! Mom then excused herself for a short while. Steve talked to us and gave all of us some scratches and rubs. He was very comfortable and a bit nervous, I sensed from him, but not a bad kind of nervous, just something like I was sensing from mom earlier, and she still had a little going on still. Interesting! When she returned, the muzzle was taken off me, which I was very grateful for. I surely didn't like that thing. Guess, I would have to behave myself if I didn't want it on again. It was just hard at times for me to control myself. Mom told Steve she was working on my aggression and said she was sorry that he had to experience it, that something bad for sure had happened to me in the past to make me this way, and she was going to help me to stop behaving in this manner. He seemed to understand, and they talked about this together while mom placed the flowers in a container. They did smell yummy!

Mom and Steve were seeing a lot of each other. It was also getting very busy around here with things being taken away and other funny weird things were being put in their place. Special kinds of music was being played many times. There was this big evergreen tree that was brought into the house and placed in the corner. That made me so happy! If I couldn't get outside, then I guess they brought one in for me to use. *Wow! This family is great. Who else would do such a thing!* I thought. Well, after a while, it was a good thing that they didn't understand my true thinking. You see, and as you probably already know, it wasn't for me personally or for Benjamin or even Pickles to climb on. It was for this holiday thing and a very special person they told us who is called Jesus Christ. It was called Christmas and to celebrate his birthday and memory. I just couldn't understand why they did this when I never saw him come to celebrate with us over the many years I was with them. Never, not even once did he come! This one really got me for sure, yep, just didn't understand this human celebration thing they did for him. But I have to admit, I always did get very special presents from them during this time, so did Benjamin and Pickles—lots of treats and chew toys. So this, Jesus, person must be someone really special, to do all this for! I sure would like to meet him.

We all had great fun during these holidays. Steve and I had something in common. It was our first holiday season, as they called it, that we were both experiencing it together with family. Actually, this was my first holiday season celebration anywhere. Steve became a very special person in our lives who spent much time with us. We all seemed to like him a lot. He gave Pickles and Benjamin special time as well. What a really nice human!

CHAPTER 34

Loved

To step back a little, the very first holiday I celebrated with them was an interesting new lesson. Before this Christmas holiday, there was this one that was called Thanksgiving. Wait till you hear this one! Anyway, during these holidays, many humans would make all different kinds of food, special treats, and desserts for themselves. Well, this one particular time, after mom had made her special pies, cookies, and other goodies, she placed most of them on a nice long tabletop dresser higher than I could reach easily. What I could see sure looked tasty and smelled so good! I wondered which one would be for me? But Mom said we were to stay away from them.

When all was cleaned up, they seemed to be in a hurry to get to a thing called a movie. After they all left, our home was now quiet, which gave the rest of us time to run and have much fun playing with one another until, that is, I found myself near the goodies. Gosh, they smelled so good. I lifted myself up on the edge with my front paws to get a closer look. Each one had a special smell. So good they were! But as I searched, I still wondered which one was for me. I continued until I heard Benjamin coming, so back to playing I went.

Well! Guess what happened? When we heard them coming home, we all went back to our sleeping areas to lay down. They were all so happy coming in and doing lots of talking to each other. Mom decided to make some coffee, as they seemed to do a lot, and asked the others who wanted some pie. I went over to greet her, and as she turned to pet me, she noticed with a surprised look and asked in a rather deep stern voice.

"Jake, what is that all over your face?"

It was kind of funny at the time but only for a few seconds. Her facial expression changed from a curious, wondering look to a look of "Oh no, what did you do now!" look.

At that very moment, Barrett said, "Mom, you had better come in here!"

When mom went to Barrett, where all the pies were lined up, she said in a very loud voice, "Jake! What have you done to my pies? Jake! You come over here this minute!"

I went rather reluctantly, and she looked at me with such a sad, somewhat angry, frustrated expression. She could only look at me and couldn't say a thing, not a thing! I wasn't sure if that was bad or not.

What did I do? All these delicious-smelling pies and desserts were just sitting there right in the open for me to check out! Really, they were! Couldn't I have some too? They always shared with us. Did I taste that particular one before I was allowed to? I looked at her with such questioning eyes and wonder that she only turned away from me and told me to go lay down. I did as I was told, but still, I just didn't understand what I did wrong?

I found out later that the one I really enjoyed was her twice-a-year special meringue pies she makes during these holiday times. I could understand too that it was special. I really enjoyed it a lot. But thank goodness for me, I guess, that she always made more than one of this kind. I did eat a lot of it. Aw, come on! If you had tasted it too, you would have understood why I ate that one. It was really good, and I think I would have eaten more if Benjamin hadn't interrupted me. It was so good! What a treat it was too! Yes, I did learn that I shouldn't taste the pies. From then on, she always made a very small one just for me. It was her special lemon meringue pie. (Benjamin and Pickles weren't interested in these pies at all.) This became a tradition each time she baked them. After all, it was a special family holiday celebration with all these yummy foods.

While I am on the subject of eating things that I shouldn't have, there were a few times besides this pie eating episode that I did. Of course, I guess I wasn't supposed to do it then either! Really, I'm curious and forget myself. So how could I possibly not get myself into these situations?

One day, as I was wondering around the house, I found myself in Barrett's room where he had some things lying around that I was attracted to. He had a particular ball that I found to be most interesting. After all, it was a ball, and who wouldn't want to play with it, right? So I took it out of his room and brought it downstairs. When I dropped it, it went away from me, so I went after it. It was fun for a while getting it and chasing it. Then I decided to lay down, and because it had such a nice feeling when I bit down on it, I decided to try to bite harder and harder. Then something didn't feel right when I bit on it really hard, which happened to be the last time that I was able to bite on it at all. You see, it wasn't a ball anymore. It went flat! I guess I bit a little too hard. I left it there; after all, what was I to do? There was nothing left of it, and I was very curious to find other things to play with. So I went back upstairs into Barrett's room again to find that other thing that attracted me before the ball! It had a slight smell to it and was in some kind of a box sitting in another kind of an open box. It took a bit, but I finally got my teeth on it. It was smaller than I thought but had a very nice feel to it. There was a taste to it that I never before tasted, and I kind of liked it. So downstairs I went. My mouth was beginning to have a funny feeling and taste to it after a while, and soon whatever I had was no more. All gone! Barrett's room was full of fun things, so back upstairs I went where I found some funny kind of shiny thing. I thought it was some shiny toy that made this funny noise when I used my paw to push down on it. Then it fell apart! So I decided to leave it alone, leaving many pieces behind. When I could not find anything else attractive to play with, I went back downstairs.

It was sometime before mom came home. Benjamin and I ran over to the door to greet her. We were so happy to have her home. She came in talking to us, petting us as best as she could while carrying many things. Once she placed all the things down and turned to actually pay attention to us, she came to a dead stop, took a look at me, of course, had this funny look on her face, again!

"Jake, what is on your tongue and mouth? What the heck. It is all black! Are you feeling well? Benjamin, come here," she said. "Are you okay?" she asked as she proceeded to check him out.

She then checked my body and just couldn't understand why I had a black tongue and some on my face. Mom decided to check out the rooms, and when she came to the big room, the family room, she called out very loudly, again, "Jake!"

It wasn't the kind of Jake calling that sounded happy either! Oh, what did I do now! She just stood there, looked at the floor. It was actually the tan wall to wall carpeting that had these big black puddling stains on many places. I didn't pay much attention to them at the time. But when I went over to the room and saw the big spots, I saw the difference from before to now. Mom now understood what happened. She looked at me, spoke very firmly, and held back her anger toward me. What a mess, it was.

I could tell she was not happy with me at all. I was a bit nervous at this point. She went down the list of all the things I had done, and then she said, "This one tops it, Jake! What is this and where did you get it?"

She told me to go onto my bed and to stay there. After she examined the carpeting with the black stuff and tried to clean it up, it was hardly coming off, I heard her say. She decided to go and search the rest of the house.

She came downstairs after a while holding the shiny things and some other stuff, showing them to me, and said; "Jake, this is bad. You destroyed a project that Barrett was working on. He is not going to be happy with you as I am not happy with you at this moment! I hope and pray you didn't swallow any of this aluminum foil. Yet I don't know how much there was to begin with. What you have on your tongue is some kind of ink. I just don't know what kind it is? Oh, Jake! I'll have to keep a close eye on you. Jake, you sure are a handful, and to keep you out of trouble from now on, you will have to be gated in this area when we are not home. Do you understand what you did, Jake? I tried to give you some freedom due to your past experiences, but I guess it was too soon. You will have to learn the hard way what you should and should not be doing. We will start this as soon as I get the gates out of the attic, Jake. I have never had to gate any of my pets till you. You sure are a handful! Now in the meantime, I will have to figure out how to get these deep black spots out of my carpeting."

Well, as the days went on, Mom worked tirelessly on each and every spot till she got every spot out of the carpet. What a great job she did too! You couldn't tell what had happened. Now, when Barrett found out what I had done to his stuff, he came over and brought me to his room, said many things to me, and I was never to go into his room again. For a few days, he couldn't or wouldn't talk to me. I tried to go over to him whenever he was there to say I'm sorry by trying to get him to pet my head. I would put my nose under his hand or arm and move it. He just looked at me and said to leave him alone for now, to go away. Boy, that really hurt me, and I just felt so sad for a few days. Barrett stayed away from me for a while, and then a few days later, he finally came over to me and said that he forgave me. But because of what I did to his project, he was not able to meet his deadline and lost an opportunity for something. Whatever that all meant, I didn't understand. All I knew at that moment was that he was not angry with me. I was truly happy with this connection again. Even though I was being locked in the kitchen foyer area whenever they left, it was much better than being ignored. I love them so, and I know they love me too!

Another time, when they all went away for overnight, mom's friend came over to put me out. I ran upstairs and peed all over the bedding. Her friend was so mad now having to wash everything. You see, I ran onto the bed to be closer to mom's scent and then couldn't hold myself. I was a little mad that I wasn't with Mom, too.

With all these things that I did, I must tell you something—one thing that really did scare me. I would hear people telling Mom to get rid of me because of all the things I would damage. I do love this home and family. What if I am so bad that they tie me outside like Daddy Joe did and no one would find me? No one would care for me, love me, or I love them? Being all alone again in scary dark

places, dirty, and fighting with others for food or a place to sleep—
this really scared me. Would they do this to me? I had to believe
no! Because Mom would answer them firmly, saying that whatever I
had been through before, if she got rid of me, then she would be no
different from those who treated me badly. Also, I was part of this
family, and I would have to learn like anyone. In fact, they would all
have to learn to be patient, understanding, being more aware of their
things, and in time, I would be just fine. Besides, I am a great pet
who just has some issues. After all, who doesn't have issues? Patience,
understanding, and training is what they are doing for me and for us!
Yep, mom is amazing, and she always makes me feel so very special
and loved.

CHAPTER 35

Countertop

As the years went on, we grew together and became such a great family. Oh sure, I still did do some of those no-nos, but not as often—just every once in a while no matter how much I tried! I just couldn't help myself.

Like this one time, mom was making some kind of a delicious meal in the kitchen, and she had some food on the countertop. The house smelled so good with whatever she was making. I had hoped that I would be getting some. (Why, you ask, should we be getting table food instead of dog food? You see, dalmatians have to be careful of getting too much of a certain kind of protein, so back then, Mom would make a lot of our food. Some protein specifically called "purines"—it's an organic compound that causes too much uric acid and, in humans, something called gout. Wow! Being in this place is amazing how I remember things and how smart I seem to be! Right? Who knew and who would have remembered this stuff? Although, I heard mom say this many times to people, explaining about caring for guys like us.)

Anyway, to get back, Mom was busy in the kitchen. She was also walking back and forth into the other room where Steve was doing some work. She returned very quickly and seemed a bit confused. She went looking on the countertop for something, went to the refrigerator a couple of times, then back to the countertop. She asked Steve if he had seen the mozzarella for the pizza she was making because she was sure that she put the block of cheese on the counter to shred before she went into the room. Of course, I was lying on the floor not too far from there, minding my own business. Then Mom looked at me, back to the countertop, and to me again.

Her eyes widened, and she made this weird face, and in a loud stern voice, she said, "Oh, Jake, you didn't? You couldn't have eaten the whole two-pound block of cheese in this short of a time! Two-pounds, Jake?" She paused then continued, "But you did, didn't you? Jake! You stinker. You just ate my topping for our pizza!"

I was getting blamed for this, and you know what? Mom was right. I did eat it! It took me one quick jump to get it off and a few big bites to swallow it almost whole. Gosh, it was one of the best cheeses I ever had! Guess, I am not only a fast runner but a quick jumper and eater! Yet Mom wasn't so happy even if I did enjoy it. When I saw her face, I felt bad. But I couldn't do anything about it then. So, I did my best to never do it again.

There was one other time after this, after a long time in between, that I managed to get some goodies. We had moved to another house, and in the kitchen on both sides of the kitchen sink were some side shelves, three to be exact on each side. Steve bought Mom some flowers and some goodies that were in a pretty red box with a special shape they would call heart-shaped. Anyway, before they went out for a special dinner, mom decided to put the box up high onto the second shelf to keep away from us. It was up high with the countertop not having much space between the top cabinets as well as the two sinks being right there. Oh well! Now the interesting part is when they both came home. Did you guess what was coming? Yep, on the floor was the box torn apart, and all the wonderful good-ies inside were gone—right down into our bellies! I did get to it, and boy, I don't know what they were, but oh my, yummy, yummy, and yummy! Ben had some too! You do know that I could smell them through the box even that high up? Mom and Steve were amazed at how I got the box. They never did figure out how I did it. But I did! Mom looked at me, and of course, she knew right away it was me.

She said, "Jake, how the heck did you get those chocolates? Just how? They were six feet or so off the floor and above the countertop? Jake, you are a wonder and amazing! Just how did you do this? Is there nothing safe from you? What did you do? Get Benjamin to stand there while you climbed onto his back? Also, thank goodness they were milk chocolate and not dark chocolate. Yet we will still need to keep an eye on all of you."

So with all this information given to you, I am going to leave you with a mystery to see if you could ever figure out how I managed to get the box down from that tiny high shelf above the countertop.

CHAPTER 36

Step Potato

One of our outings.

You do have to understand that there were many times we just enjoyed ourselves as a family by going out for wonderful car rides (and ones that always brought me back home). There was always a tiny little speck of nervousness whenever we went for a car ride for the longest time. I managed to get over it and always felt very secure being with this family. No matter what, we were a wonderful family. Ben and I would get to go running in the woods, playing that hide-and-seek game with Mom. So much fun! The hikes up the mountain and being put into the canoes was always an interesting adventure. That fresh air and open space was wonderful as well. I think this was always one of my special great memories being on the water. It was so peaceful, floating with the fresh air coming into my nostrils. Mom and another doing the paddling while Ben and I got to look around, and every now and then, we would get to jump into the water for a refreshing swim. But always, we had our life vests on for sure. Mom never took that chance again.

On one adventure trekking through the woods, we encountered another human male who had a smaller dog than Ben and myself. We wanted to say hi to him, so finally, mom took us closer. But when I got closer, I took a nip at him very quickly to everyone's surprise. I did it because I sensed he was going to nip at me first. I didn't hurt him much. He did yelp once, and a little something started to come out the side of his nose. The young male quickly ran away with his dog. Mom was upset and embarrassed, she talked to Steve. Then she tried to go after the young male and offer any financial assistance that might incur. After all, she had to do that much, but the young male was gone.

Mom looked at me and asked me, "Jake, what has gotten into you? Why do we always need to be on guard with you? Why?"

But, Mom, he was going to nip at me. I was just protecting myself! She didn't understand this part.

From then on, we seemed to stay clear from pets and people until she did some special training with me, again. In time, I was able to go near others without any incident. I was able to understand my behavior and took heed to Mom's love and training. Yet I still did do some heavy barking before people were to come into our home to be sure they wouldn't hurt anyone in my home. I always sniffed them up and down just to be sure.

Now it was interesting that during these particular times, mom decided to get that invisible fencing she had talked about long ago, especially after I chased some pretty interesting creatures that took me into the deeper woods. The only great thing about the invisible fence for my part was that after all that Mom did, it backfired. I became so sad about having that shocking experience on my neck it made me so afraid to go outside at all! It would hurt my sensitive neck, and I was becoming very depressed as I heard them say. Even inside, I just wasn't my happy self anymore. After they got it, sometime later, I ran after a deer who had no trouble going farther than I could go. I ran after her so fast it took me right through the invisible fence line where I got stuck and realized, oh no! I tried to get back and turned around, got that hard shock again and again and again as I turned in circle after circle, trying to get away but just couldn't. It got me so upset and confused as to how to get back safely onto my own side. Finally, Mom and Dean came running toward me and helped me get out of my situation. Never again did I do that!

From then on, I didn't want to go outside, let alone leave the front step. So Mom would say to me that I had become a step potato instead of a couch potato. It didn't matter what she said at that moment because no matter what, I wasn't going to go anywhere when I went outside, especially on my own, not even to do my business. So I had to be encouraged to go outside with the leash on every time. Even though mom decided that this invisible fence would be turned off immediately, it still took a very long time for me to trust going outside off the step. Being walked around the borderline and around our house showed me where I could go. Even though this was done before and during the invisible fence training, it didn't stop me from running after the other creatures. Yet the memory of that last experience getting stuck and shocked, ouch, over and—ouch—over and—ouch—over again, I paid much more attention to this training again. It was a very sad time for me, but with this newer experience in time, I was able to be off leash in the yard while my family members were with me. It was a wonderful feeling, and I began to be myself again, happy and carefree.

Now you have to understand that my experience with this invisible fence is a rare thing. Most other pets who have been on the invisible fence training do very well. I was the rare case that just couldn't handle the collar and the whole experience from it. But then again, after having that awful experience of getting shocked over and over, then not wanting to leave the step, I guess you can say, in a matter of speaking or barking, that the invisible fence did keep me on the property. It had its purpose. Then for sure, after the third round of boundary training took place, I also stopped being a total step potato!

CHAPTER 37

Oh, Pickles

Pickles always keeping a secret eye on everything.

Well, you know, even though I tell a lot about myself, and this is, after all, my story (right?), I would like to tell you about our Pickles. Now Pickles was a funny rare cat. He was a stinker, as they would say, who would like to scare people more than I did with my barking at the door. You see, he liked to hide then jump out at them and grab their leg while giving a little nip. If you had your hand on the doorknob going outside with him hiding in the room somewhere, while you were talking to another human and he thought you were going to open the door, you got him coming after you for sure. Now mind you, it didn't matter if you thought he wanted to go outside or not (he was not ever allowed out anyway) or even if you didn't ever see him there, you were going to get it no matter what! Gotta admit, those times I did see this happen, it was kind of funny to see those reactions from the humans, and oh boy, the things that came out of their mouth! That was even funnier from what I could understand. The things I didn't understand were just as funny. Pickles would snicker a lot afterward and walk around with his tail so high and straight up the air for such a long time.

Yet there was this one time he did get out, and everyone went crazy looking for him in the woods. Let me tell you too, there were lots and lots of woods around, which made it very hard to know where he might have gone or if he was still alive! Finally, after many, many hours of worry and looking with no one being able to sleep either, it was very late in the middle of the night, we could hear him meowing. He sounded so scared. The woods were strange at night with all the noises. Everyone went out to look for him, yelling, calling, searching. They were all scared for him. Finally, he slowly came to Barrett. Pickles was more his cat anyway. He just loved him for all his quirks and character. Barrett almost cried when Pickles came very slowly and unsure of things toward him. They were all wearing gloves and long sleeves, not sure of what they might find on Pickles or even if they did find him at all! The gloves were to keep any germs or diseases off the human skin so they wouldn't get sick and maybe die. I could hear a lot of what they said. Pickles was a mess with dirt, wet spots, some scratches like he was in a fight or so. It was smart for them to wear the gloves for protection. So after some rest, he calmed down from his experience. Mom and Barrett cleaned him up, and for the next three weeks or so, he had to be kept in a private room to be sure he didn't carry this thing called rabies. I guess having rabies can be pretty bad from what I heard them saying. After the three weeks of time and Pickles going a bit nuts staying in the private room, he was able to come out and play again with us. Poor guy, it took him many days to get back to himself. He had himself a very bad time in the woods, he told Ben and me. Something was after him, and he was able to get away just in time. It wasn't like the kind of after him that Ben and I would do during our play. Pickles just knew the difference;

therefore, he never wanted to be in that situation again. I, of course, understood the situation and comforted him as much as I could. It is very, very scary to be chased after by someone or something that wants to harm you, which makes me have this very special bond with Pickles and Ben. Even though I have and do cause Ben some issues, I would always be there to protect him as well—always I would for both of them!

So anyway, it really didn't matter whether or not he really wanted to go out. It was just the fact that they were near the door, and if they opened it, he might somehow have gotten out and wouldn't be able to get back inside quickly before anyone knew he was gone. So by jumping up at their hand and nipping or scratching it, scaring them as well, they let go of the handle, and he felt safe again that they weren't going to open the door. It was just his way! No one seemed to understand his reasoning for doing that, but I did. It was like, "Get your hand off the door, and please don't open it, for I might find myself outside, scared, alone, and chased after to be hurt or worse." Get it now? (So please always pay attention to your pets. There are good reasons why we do things that you think are strange or mean! There are always two sides to a situation, you know!)

During our times together, as I've said, there's a special bond we shared, and we just loved each other so much. As time went on, Pickles was getting on in years. He was older than Benjamin and me. Up until the last few days he was with us, he seemed to be getting a bit slower and wanted to be left alone, except for Barrett to comfort him. Then one day, Barrett went in to see him and found him to be so quiet and almost still with breath. Barrett called us all in as we stayed with Pickles till he took his last breath. Oh, the tears came from all, and those last words spoken to him were, "Oh, Pickles!"

CHAPTER 38

Life Taking a Turn

Jake, Benjamin and Me.—2005

Mom was going out a lot lately. Even though she always came back, thank goodness, this always affected me. It didn't seem to matter how long she left. I just always felt a sadness, along with feeling a bit upset. I missed her so much.

I remember a few times missing her so much that when Steve would sleep over, he always found me sleeping on her side of the bed. I know when she would call and talk to him because he would put the phone by my ear, and I could hear her voice. That brought me such happiness. The first time I heard it, it was a bit like, "What is this all about? I hear mom, but where is she? Why does this thing have Mom inside of her? Did it eat her? Why was she hiding? But she always sounded happy, so I guess it was okay." It was like the time I thought my one brother was inside that mirror until I found out it was my very own refection. Remember that one? I did understand this to be a telephone, as I was told. I just didn't quite get that whenever it made this ring sound, someone would always pick it up and start talking, or they would pick it up and do things to it then start talking without it ever ringing. What made it hard is that I never could see who it was. But Steve would always give me the phone when it was mom so I could hear her voice and words but just couldn't ever see her!

So this one night, while Mom was away, Steve woke up with such a surprise of seeing me sitting on the telephone while it was on the nightstand table thing! Yep, I was sitting on the phone! I figured if they could pick it up at different times and do something to talk, then maybe if I sat on it, I could get Mom to talk to me sooner. Really, this did happen! I missed her so much!

Now just a little off topic here. This is the perfect time for me to take a moment to mention something to you personally. You see, the one thing that could help us, you know, guys like us, your pets and also your outside animals, they have so many feelings, so much understanding, and so much love to give, is, if humans would really understand how important it is to let us pets know when you are going away no matter for how long or short. It helps us to prepare for a time without you and what to expect. Yes, even though mom did this all the time, I still felt lonely without her no matter how long she was gone. But the most important thing was that she gave me a warning that she was going. Honestly, this does make it easier, just not perfect!

There was another time when mom went away only, and these special people came to our home. I would get put into the garage to stay for a while until those people looking at our home left. Mom would leave her Jeep parked inside with the window open on the side that she could get in and out by the wall. It was a tight fit getting in and out, but it worked. I didn't like staying in the garage by myself, and I could smell the wonderful scent of mom from within the car, especially on that one side. Now the problem was that I needed to be closer to that scent. I finally figured it out. Even though it was a very tight fit with the wall being so very close to the door with the open window, I struggled and struggled to lift myself inside the car. I did get a little belly hurt from the part of the door where I had to climb inside of it. That big round thing that mom put her hands on made it a bit harder, but I used the wall for my back legs to get me up and over. It sure was such a struggle, but I finally got in! The really funny part of it was that Dean thought that Steve put me in the car, and Steve thought that Dean put me in the car. They were so funny trying to figure out how I got into the car, but I did! Later, they did find some scratches next to the outside handle on the car. Oops, I hope I wouldn't upset mom for doing that when she gets home.

Mom was told about what I did and how much I was missing her. Also, I wasn't eating much either. I sure was very unhappy when she went away. I had a very special bond with her. She always talked to me, to Ben, and Pickles as well. We went places with her. She gave us so many hugs and kisses, played with us, brushed us, which felt so nice, made special food for us, sat, and very quietly spent time with us in the other realm—my realm of understanding things better. She didn't say many words but used her thoughts to communicate with us. I just loved that!

So anyway, when she did come home and we were ready to all go out together, the car wouldn't start. When someone finally came to help get it started again, she noticed that the special light nearest to the big window on top came on and the other one was still off. So she figured out how the car/Jeep wouldn't start. You see, I hit my head on the one light, and it stayed on all the time while I was in there. I heard her say something like, "That's how the battery got drained. Jake hit his head on the light." Anyway, that was another one of the times that I did something but didn't get into trouble, nor did I get into trouble for the scratches I left on the door by the outside handle in order to climb in. Boy, am I one lucky dog!

Now as time went with this wonderful family, life was really good for me. They all said I was such a great dog. I was happy and pretty healthy too! But things don't always go as we might think they should. Looking back, I thought that the invisible fence time was a very sad time for me. But being in this particular time was even sadder. I wasn't afraid, but life ahead from then on was the most difficult time for me. So I'll tell you why. You see, it started one day when mom found this lump just to the left of my tail based on my backside. I could sense that Mom didn't like this one bit. What was going on? I wondered. Apparently, at this point, this was not going to turn out to be good for any of us. For you see, life was taking a turn.

CHAPTER 39

Loved Me As Well

Mom kept checking that particular spot on my backside as I just kept licking and biting at it as much as I could. It was annoying and bothered me. I could feel my skin pulling and tugging. It was driving me kind of nuts. Mom would take me into the car for a ride to see a special person who always would check out my backside by my tail. Mom and Steve were sad, I could tell. When Dean and Barrett were around me, they seemed to be different. It was like a heavier kind of sad emotion. Everyone seemed to be trying to always make me happy and treated me with even more attention than I could have ever imagined could be possible. Ben and I would continue our play as usual.

Now this one day, mom took me to see that special person again, a vet, he was called. The thing on my backside was getting so very big, and he needed to do some work on me, mom had told me.

I didn't know at that time that I would be staying there by myself, and this scared me that I was being left behind. I couldn't believe this was happening, but mom kept reassuring me that I was going to be going home with them the next day. This was my turn to be away for a while from home. I couldn't stand being left behind. It did kind of remind me of the place I had been to before I met Dean and went to live with them. So it wasn't as bad as it could have been. But to be left behind made me very sad. I just kept remembering mom's words that I would be home tomorrow. Mom had some water from her eyes when she left. I wanted to run to her and lick her face, but I couldn't. The female who worked there put me into a cage. I could only see mom's loving face. Her eyes were so very sad but filled with love as well. I just didn't know why or what was going on.

I waited, but for what, I didn't know. For sure, though, I was getting hungry and thirsty. Then the female came back, let me out of the cage and took me to a special room. As she spoke softly to me, I felt something going into my leg; it pinched a little. I also remember feeling a little sleepy very shortly after that pinch. But I still could remember that she and another male lifted me onto a high table. Wow, what is going on? That's all I remembered.

When I woke, I felt so weird and confused. Like long ago from that first time when I meet the two-legged creatures, known as humans, I found myself in a similar situation now. I had things attached to my leg as I lay on a comfortable bed inside a closed cage. One thing for sure was that, this time, I wasn't going to be so afraid. I had more of an understanding. Something must have been done to me in order for me to be like this. That much was for sure.

The female human who took me out of the cage was called Janice. She checked on me many times throughout the day. There were others who also came to see me. I was beginning to feel great pain in my backside area. When this would occur, the humans would give me something, and I would feel better. You know, all I really wanted to do was to go home. Mom said it would only be overnight. So where is she?

Sometime later, Janice came over and took out all the things attached to me. I did feel a bit weak and only ate a little bit. I couldn't hold much down, you know. I was also so glad to get that stuff off, and this meant that I would be leaving soon. It was later in the day that Mom finally came for me. I was so happy to see her, and Dean was with her too!

I had to wear this head thing that was going to keep me from biting at the bandages on my backside—like that was going to stop me! You're right. You know, and you guessed it! This was one thing that was not going to stay on for too long. No way, no how! I couldn't stand things on my neck and head that kept me from doing the things I liked or needed to do. I felt so helpless.

When we got home, mom made me a little something to eat. I just couldn't eat much at that time, but the broth she made seemed to help me. She was so loving toward me and the others, of course.

As I lay on my bed, I could feel something that was a bit painful, itching, and most annoying on my backside. So you got it! I tried with all my might to reach that area to bite at what was causing my problem. After some tries, without success, and Mom warning me not to touch it many times, I decided that I would tug and tug at this collar thing till it came off my head. It took some time, but I got it off, as well as those bandages on my backside. Oh boy! It felt so good to get into it and bite those itches. Everything was feeling great, until—yep, mom came by to check on me and stopped in her tracks. She had a look of horror and "oh no" on her face. She came rushing over to me, gathered up my collar, and managed to get it back on my neck. This time, she did something that made it harder for me to get off again. I guess, I did something to my stitches that I shouldn't have done. She was saying all kinds of things with great concern as she cleaned up the mess, trying to stop the bleeding that I caused myself. She said out loud that I dug a hole deeper than she had seen before and begged me to not to do it again. With some hard work on her part and the Vet, they were able to make everything right on me. With all that struggling on my part and repairing what I did to myself, I sure was tired. So off to a wonderful sleep I went, even if the head thing was not very comfortable for me.

The days went by, and a few visits back to the place that did my surgery, the vets, I was finally able to get that head thing off! Now mom kept checking that lump on my backside. She, along with Steve, Barrett, and Dean were not very happy. It took many weeks when it started coming back and growing faster, along with a couple more little surgeries.

After another visit to the vet, mom was told to take me to see a specialist. So off on another trip we went, and this time, it was a very long ride. Boy, you wouldn't believe this place. It was big, and I saw others similar to me being led around, who didn't seem to feel so good themselves. I felt pretty great, except for that annoying thing on my backside, so why did I need to be here? At this place, we waited for a bit then saw this big male who was the head veterinarian, Mom was telling Steve. Staying there for a while was very tiring for me. The vet person took me to another room where they placed me on a table and kept looking at my backside. They touched it, looked at it, and I felt some pinching, which didn't seem to bother me too much while they did what they needed to do. Then finally, I went back to see Mom and Steve. There was so much talking I could only pick up on a few words like blood, lump, cancer, keeping me there for months, and being able to visit me. I couldn't pick up on much more after hearing "keeping me there for months and visiting me"? Mom and Steve were saying to the vet man that me being there alone without mom would make me very depressed, and that alone would kill me. Now what did they mean by "kill me"? It sounded serious, but I wasn't going to let that keep me from being with mom. Then again, what choice did I have?

After sometime we left, Mom and Steve didn't seem to feel any better. Their energy was heavier, quieter, and more serious. I was in the back in my crate, and all I wanted to do was to go to them to let them know everything is okay. I am here for them. I wanted to lick them and hug them. But all I could do was sense their pain and sadness. I could only lay there helpless, but the long ride home gave me a chance to sleep most of the way, even with all the bumps, along with the many short stops and goes. Finally, it got much better once we left that very busy place with so many houses of all kinds and sizes, humans, cars, noises, and those strange smells. It was so nice to be back at home.

Mom and everyone else who came to see me seemed a bit different from then on. I did get to go outside as always, got some very special tasty treats, and lots of extra pets with scratches. I do have to admit that there seemed to be times that I didn't feel quite like myself. Things were beginning to feel different for me at times. Most of the time, I felt great. But that lump kept getting bigger, and it was beginning to not just annoy me as I tried to bite at it, but it was also becoming raw as it was eating at my skin and deeper within. I sometimes was having trouble going to do my poop. I didn't always want to eat as much anymore. But I did always want the loving, and it helped me lots. It took my worries away as I comforted those who loved me as well.

CHAPTER 40

Needed to Stop

I'm not feeling all that great now.

I remember this one particular time when Mom had just gotten home from being away for a short time. Barrett and Dean wanted her to go with them to see some parade. But for some reason, mom insisted that she really didn't want to go away from me this day. Well, it's a good thing she didn't go with them because not long after my human brothers left, I was standing by the door, waiting to go outside, and as mom came by, she started to scream very loudly for Steve who was in that room where the water runs a lot, and they lay in the big tub thing. Anyway, I had no idea why she was screaming so loudly for him. Something about getting her towels. She was trying to hold onto me and doing something to my backside at the same time. All I know was that I saw a lot of red stuff coming down my leg, all over the floor, and some on the walls. What could have been going on? I was getting a bit concerned, confused, and feeling somewhat weaker and scared as well. Steve came running out, mom told him to get towels and to press hard onto my backside. She ran to that phone thing, and I heard her ask for the vet. She told Steve that he had to come in special due to the holiday. Mom ran out, got the Jeep car, and both of them tried to take care of my backside while Steve carried me to the car. He drove while Mom stayed with me in the back and held my backside with many towels. When we got there, to mom's surprise, the vet was waiting for us. Then everything happened so fast. The next thing I was being brought into a special room, felt a pinch again, and lifted onto a table. That's all I remember.

When I woke up, I was in a cage with things on my legs. Again! Boy, this was happening to me a lot! However, this time, I felt so very weak and sick. They took care of me for many hours before mom came to see me. They said to her that I could go home now. That made me so very happy. There is nothing like being home no matter how much care someone else gives to you. It is home that makes me feel better for faster healing. Do you know what I mean? Anyway, before we left, I heard mom talking to the vet.

She asked him something like, "What did you have to do to, Jake?"

He said that he had to cut, tie, and cauterize so much that he lost track. That's one thing I remember most but didn't understand. He said to her also that it wasn't going to get any better, and there wasn't much more he could do. I could see Mom's heart energy shift so quickly from concern to a very heavy deep pain of some kind. I just didn't understand what it was all about. What was going to get worse? What was the cutting, tying, and cauterizing about? I felt fine, expect for being weak and a bit sick in my stomach area just like I always feel after having things like this done to me! But it wasn't me that I was concerned about, as it was more for Mom. I couldn't bear to see her like this. Was it my fault that she was so heavy in her heart? Did I cause this heart energy pain? What could I have done? I must try to make her happy. When she came nearer to me, I reached out and gave her a lick on her face. I was surprised to see the water come from her eyes as she hugged me for such a long time. I could also feel her deep love and a little lifting of the heaviness she had held.

At home, mom kept changing my bandages, and I had to wear that big head thing again for some time. We didn't get too much company anymore, except for this one time—there were two females that came to our home. It was a long time since I had done anything like this. I ran and jumped onto the door. This caused the older female to be so scared of me that she didn't want to come in. Mom took me to the other room and went back for them to come in. After a few minutes, I went over to the older female who was sitting on the long, soft sofa, as it was called, to lay my head down on her lap. She was so scared, surprised, and startled. Mom had been talking to her and noticed that I was letting her know that she was accepted by me, that I liked her, and also that I was sorry for scaring her so much. This made her feel more comfortable, and she started to pet me very gently. It was good to have her do this to me and that I made her feel happier. This was important that I could help her feel better. She seemed to carry a special sadness within her, and I could sense that her life energy was very little. I liked her. That was the first and only time I had ever seen this older female.

After they left, mom spoke to me about my scaring her and that I wasn't to do that again to her or anyone else. It wasn't nice to do. So do you want to guess what I did from that time on? Come on. Take a guess. Okay, did you figure out that I did it again or not? If you said "not," then you were right! Even though I had been talked to many times about this before, I took great care not to scare anyone like that again. It was just something that I finally needed to stop.

CHAPTER 41

Alone for a While

2005—Hi, Dean,
I'm still here.

2005—Yes, I'm
ready, it's time.

Over the next few months, I had gone back to the vet and had surgery done again. This time, the vet told Mom and Steve that there
is absolutely nothing more that can be done. It is too much of the
cancer taking over and that I should be put down. Now mom was
told by many other people to put me down, but all she would say is
that "he's not ready. He will let me know when it is his time!"

Mom was supposed to go away again but decided to stay with
me. For as much as she wanted to go to the great work she did, she
knew that family was more important. As I lay on a cozy, comfortable bed on the floor in the living room, mom would come from
around the corner to peek in on me, and she didn't realize that I knew

she was doing this very often. She would take time to lay with me as well, talk to me, and hold me. After many times of her doing this, the one time she peeked in on me, I lifted my head and looked right at her. She took a quick peek at me then left. However, in a split second, she popped back, looked right at me, eye to eye, we connected silently, and asked, "It's time, Jake?"

I noted to her in our special way, she understood that it was time, and I could no longer bear the pain that was getting so strong. I was feeling so very weak and that I loved her so much.

She immediately called the vet to come over to do something instead of me going for a car ride to them. That she wanted me to be home. She then called Steve, Barrett, and Dean. Dean was too far away to be home that night. She started to clear things out and put things in the room. Steve and Barrett came over as soon as they could. Not long after, the vet came to our home. Mom almost told the vet to leave that she wasn't going to do this to me. But she stopped herself, realizing that this was selfish on her part, that it was not for her that the vet was there but for me, Jake. Mom always confronted her emotions and thoughts to see what was best for the situation, even if she didn't like or approve of it. In this situation, she knew that this was in the highest and best interest for me, not her! So the vet came into the house and came over to me. She was about to examine me but didn't touch me yet when I came out with a yelp.

Mom said, "Oh, Jake, no one touched you yet. See, he does do yelps without touching him."

However, at that time, mom was so emotional that she didn't realize that this was my last yelp to give to let them know how much I loved them and how grateful I was to be with them and them with me. It wasn't a bad yelp but a yelp coming from my physical pain, my emotions that I was feeling from all of them toward me, and my greatest appreciation and love for all of them.

Mom had lit candles and played some nice music that we liked to listen to that kept me calm at other times. Barrett was on the phone with Dean while this was going on, and the vet then confirmed it was time. She gave me a little pinch of something, and then I felt some weird things going on inside of me that didn't last for very long. The next thing I knew, I was looking down at everyone, and I saw my body still on the bed. It was so still, and mom was hugging me while crying, it's called. As a matter of fact, they were all crying so much.

After some time, Mom lifted my body and took me outside to the spot she had dug on the property. Steve and Barrett had gotten me some toys and a nice blanket. I had watched this as they did so. No one seemed to know I was watching because they were so busy taking care of me that they didn't pay any attention. It was okay with me for now because I was busy watching them and how lovingly they took care of my physical body for the last time. They wrapped me in a wonderful blanket. Mom dug the hole deeper so no other wild animal could smell my remains and dig me up. Then they all placed me into the hole with some of my favorite toys wrapped within my blanket. They each took turns placing the earth on top of me and a nice flower to mark my site. Each stayed for a bit then left me and mom alone for a while.

CHAPTER 42

Again

Before it came time for my spirit body to depart completely, I knew that I wasn't quite ready to move forward just yet. I had unfinished business to take care of with Mom. You see, for as much as she understood what happens when we leave the physical body and go beyond this life, I needed to connect to her a while longer. As you know, we had this very, very special connection. Mom's open acceptance and experiences of knowing there was more than this physical life made our connection easier. Those particular times that she personally experienced with other human beings departing their physical body, not only gave her deep belief that there is more, but mostly, it confirmed this and gave her new knowledge, especially when it even came to pets and other creatures.

The first time I connected to Mom was the very morning upon her awakening on the sofa. She had stayed with Benjamin in the living room during that night to be sure he was okay with me not being there any longer. Mom took the time to comfort him. You see, this is what I mean about Mom! Even though we are pets, just dogs, or just animals to some humans, she considered us as family, that we have emotions, feelings, and are important enough. We give so much and don't ask for much back. We know and feel so very much of your thoughts, feelings, and emotions. All we want to do is make you feel better and to be happy. We have a special gift to help all humans and are here to share this with all who will accept it, that we have these very special healing powers.

Yes, we do require that we are fed, sheltered properly, and our physical, mental, and emotional needs are just as important for us as they are for humans. But again, when you are with us, our special gift is transformed into amazing comfort and healing that transcends the human condition. We are all connected to this wonderful energy.

Okay, back to Mom and Benjamin. She stayed with him to help him understand that my body was no longer with them, but my essence, my love, and my light would always be there. She placed near him my toys, held him, and talked to him about many different things until exhaustion took over, and they finally slept.

Upon her awakening, as Mom turned her head slowly to the right toward the wide opening in the foyer connecting to the living room, there she was able to see me in full view. My head appeared to her as large as the width of the double opening. I was as clear to her as if I were standing in front of her in physical form. Yet she was still able to see beyond me, through me. It was so beautiful to sense that she was not afraid at all. Although, I could sense and feel her surprise, her amazement, her joy, her disbelief that even as a pet, I could appear to her. I could sense and feel her great belief as well—slightly shocked but believing. She looked right at me with eyes wide and amazing love. Then it was my time to tell her what I needed. It was wonderful that Mom totally understood me when I told her as we connected in thought that "Mom, I am okay."

She said, "Thank you, Jake. I love you."

I felt her peace and joy. As we looked upon each other for another quick moment, I then knew for sure she was fine, so I left that particular experience.

I was able to see her for a while longer and protect her in my special way, even if she couldn't see me unless I needed her to. As the weeks followed, another time while she was busy in the privacy of her room, I came to her. (In the physical, I would push the door open and spend time with her.) Well, this time, she just seemed to know that I entered, which was so wonderful—she just knew! She turned, felt my essence next to her just like it was in the physical, and raised her hand to pet my head. Mom knew exactly where to place her hand to feel my head under her hand. Such a wonderful connection we had. It was without judgment and without doubt from her, just pure acceptance from the heart, and I could still sense that even then. She just knew when I was with her. She just knew! How beautiful this time felt for both of us. When I was in the physical, many times I would sit next to her in the front seat area while she drove. Even then, she would reach out and pet me. Well, this one particular time, while she was actually driving, she did feel my presence there and automatically reached out, placed her hand exactly upon my head as she had always done, and gave me a wonderful scratch. She knew my essence was there with her in that moment. I carried at that time a heavy energy and could sense her touching me that made this type of connection absolutely amazing!

(Note: Just to take a quick look back. As you recall in the very beginning, I started to tell you that while I was playing with my friends, I came upon a spot that made me stop. There I noted that maybe I needed to learn something, remember? Well, just maybe my looking back upon all this was not just that I had to learn something as I first thought in starting these memories. But maybe it was that mom had to share all this with you! Stop to think about this for a minute: Maybe to let you know that we all have life in some form or another no matter where; that we all have existence, we all have purpose, we all have connection, and we are all meant to be; that there is nothing by chance; that there is more; to always keep your heart and mind open; and that love goes beyond. Just maybe it was not my journey alone, but ours!)

When I knew the time had come that Mom would be truly fine, it was the time when she was outside sitting with Benjamin in the front yard pen area, talking to him and observing him. I could sense from her a sadness in her energy even though I was still connecting to her. Mom totally understood and accepted things as they truly are, yet she carried the sadness of missing me in the physical, of me playing with Benjamin, and for that matter, just being there with her. Still, it was so beautiful to see them and know the love that we all shared.

As I continued to watch, I could sense her thoughts were far off. This was the perfect time for me to let her know I was there with them. So in a special way, my energy moved toward her and, as if someone had placed their hands on either side of her face, I ever so lovingly guided her head toward the right to look up into the heavens. As she looked up, I gave her one last vision of me to say, "I am here for you always even though you already know this. That I will always be with you, loving you even from afar. But mostly, mom, that I would be here waiting for you. Yes, for you, for…when we meet again!"

IN CONCLUSION,
A NOTE FROM THE AUTHOR

My Sherry.

Pickles and Sherry
loved being together.

1999 Jake, Pickles on the sofa,
and Ben all hanging out!

You must know that in the beginning of this writing, I, the author, didn't truly know the life that Jake had experienced. However, when he came to me, except for the names and characters that I have changed along with some very minor situations, all is fact. For as we continue our story of Jake and me, I need to complete the journey of

Jake—not of this world but of the next, for what I am about to tell you is the truth!

It had been as much as a surprise to me, as it will be for you, as I tell you what truly took place. Maybe this will help you to understand more. You can then believe or not. Without a doubt, this took place! As with my unexpected human experiences, Jake assisted me to understand, believe, and prove that these beautiful and amazing experiences can and most definitely do take place with pets as well. To be more accepting, without fear, acknowledgment, and so much more that words cannot describe them. So I continue the very last experience of my Jake and his love for me in order for us, Jake and me, to share with you that life is so much more.

The following year after Jake had passed away, Benjamin, who had been by himself without any other pets, was now getting on in life. Backing up a bit, before Jake had his last days with us, I had him sitting on the sofa with me with his head on my lap. I spoke to him out loud and told him the following, "Now, Jake, I want you to understand some things. You see, for as much as I love you, you were a stinker at times of some sort. Yes, you, as you well know! You scared people out of their wits. Then you tried to let them think how loving and affectionate you were. You are, but did you have to scare them so much?"

I continued to talk to him and pet him while noting to him. "Now, Jake, I also want you to know, when it is Benjamin's time to leave here, I want you to be sure to be there for him. He is a little chicken as we know and gets scared very easily. So be sure to be there for him, okay? I also want you to know that I thank you very much for being in my life, for protecting me, loving me, for taking away my cancer as you took away my pains many time and brought them upon yourself. I love you, and I will always be here for you, no matter what, Jake, till when we meet again."

That was our true life conversation and how the title of this book came to be.

So as I mentioned, Benjamin was getting on in years, and his time was about to be exhausted. He was such a sweat, loving, goofball of a dog! We would say he was our court jester! He always brought a smile to our faces, and sometimes he would do such unexpected things, like the time we were all in the car waiting for Barrett's friend to come into the car. When Benjamin saw him coming, he jumped right over Barret and out the back seat window to run to Kevin. What a surprise to all of us! Another funny thing about him was when he would pass gas, he would smell it and then look at "us" with disgust as if we did it! He was great at playing hide-and-seek while we took long walks up the mountain or anywhere. Just a true sweetheart of a dog that made us laugh. His heart was so big and precious. Sadly, when he went out into the yard freely, we would find that he was in the neighbor's yard eating from the huge mound of cat litter that they put outside. I mean it was a huge mound about 5' high and twice as wide of litter. It should have been placed in garbage bags and properly disposed of. We found Benjamin two times eating from that cat litter mound. This we believe was the cause for his seizures. Therefore, we could no longer allow him to run freely outside. His seizures were so bad at times too! Our poor Benjamin! He suffered badly from them, and it all could have been avoided if only the neighbor properly disposed of this toxic waste. Imagine what other creatures were affected by this? Other than the seizures, Benjamin was fairly healthy for most of his life with mild issues here and there, but far in between.

It came a time that old age was taking him away from us. Again, we had a vet came to our home to prepare Benjamin for his next journey. It was very interesting because at the time when the vet was about to administer the needle, Benjamin, who had been so very weak to move, actually got up off my lap while I was sitting on the floor and turned his whole body around for easier access. It was amazing that he knew that his position in my lap was awkward for the vet to access him easily. We took our last look at each other, and it was done. Once again, we prepared Benjamin as we did Jake and placed him in the hole. However, before we placed the earth on him, something told me to go to the store and get him another toy.

I then headed out in my car down the road, to the left, and at the stop sign, something told me to look up from under my visor over the parking lot above the plaza. There in my vision up in the sky above all the stores in the plaza, I saw Jake standing there in the bliss of white. I tell you, it was the purest, clearest white one could ever see. To my surprise and astonishment, there was Jake and Pickles sitting next to each other in a full view looking toward my direction but not at me directly. (Both looked so very healthy and happy. Even though *everything* was in the purest of white on their side, I could still clearly distinguish every detail.) They were looking directly at Benjamin who had his back toward me and shaking like a leaf. Then something caught my eye off to the right in the bushes. As I looked with squinted eyes, I couldn't quite make it out at first. Then, to my surprise, it was Sherry! Oh my God, it was Sherry! My dog during the early years of Pickles and before the others were in my life. But why was Sherry there and hiding in the bushes? I later told Dean what happened and he reminded me that. Sherry and Pickles only knew each other. Then I realized, if Benjamin saw her because he was such a scaredy-cat, or dog in this case, he might not have crossed over.

Now what was so amazing was that between them was a straight dark line on the so-called ground that I could make out very clearly, almost like a divider from this side to the other. It was actually crossing over the line! The side that Benjamin was on was so dark and gloomy, like the appearance we see just before a very severe storm. As I continued to observe, I saw Jake and Pickles sitting on their side connecting to Benjamin to come across. Ben, with all his shaking, was very reluctant at first. Finally, he got up the courage to get closer to Jake. Jake extended his nose for Ben to sniff, and then he crossed over. They then sniffed each other's backsides, jumped around, and I noted that Ben was now as healthy as the others. They were happy, free, and playful. No worries, no pain, only light and love. There was so much life on that side. Then Sherry quickly came out of her hiding place. They all got to know each other. When they all turned to look at me, I actually understood them all to say, "So long. We love you. We are all fine, healthy, and happy.

See you, Mom, soon. *Just not yet!* We will all be here for you, Mom, for when we meet again."

ABOUT THE AUTHOR

RM Bryant resides in Connecticut. She is a wife and mother of three. Pets have always been a wonderful part of her life, as well as the love of the outdoors, cooking, and holistic health healing energy. This is her first published work. RM has a creative side, presently working on various writings and inventions.

CPSIA information can be obtained
at www.ICGtesting.com
Printed in the USA
LVHW051201101220
673819LV00032B/1726

9 781662 402173